PLAY

The
ASK*ing*
Game™

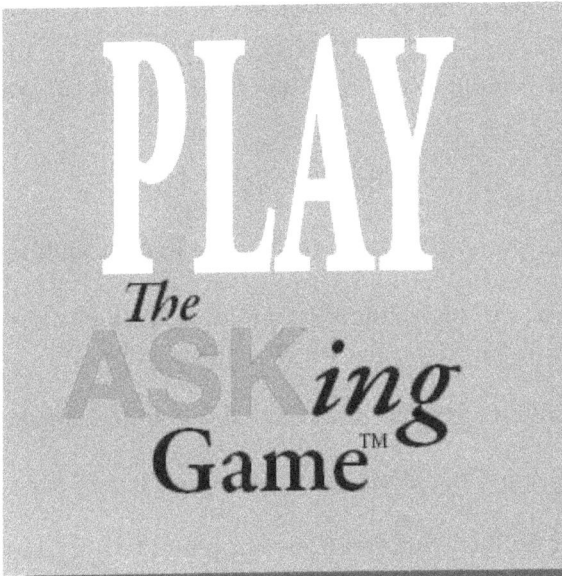

*and take the
path to what you want*

by
Wayne Rollan Melton

ASK
Play the Asking Game and take the path to what you want

Fix Bay Inc., Publishing

Fix Bay Inc and its Fix Bay Inc, Publishing are a Nevada corporation

Designed by Patty Atcheson-Melton, Wow Design Marketing, Inc.,
&
Margie Enlow, NuDirections Graphic Design Marketing

Melton, Wayne Rollan

1. Self-help 2. Self-improvement 3. Inspirational

ISBN: 978-0-9838149-8-6

Contents

The ASK*ing* Game

Dedicated to everyone who wants to learn how to truly enjoy every moment as a "great day," eager to learn how to ask for and to receive what they want from life.

Achieve YOUR Dreams

FOREWORD

Have you ever asked one question that changed the entire course of your life for the better?

Each of us can generate an amazing power to improve the quality of our lives and those of people we cherish. Sadly, though, we tend to lose track of—or never find—the best strategies to open life's proverbial treasure box filled with positive possibilities.

Herein you'll discover key, integral strategies for putting your life onto the path that your soul has always yearned to tread. Once you begin traveling along your chosen route, you'll be able to locate and enrich yourself with even more promising adventures.

For me, this change clicked into gear as a young adult, the start of my lifelong career as a graphic designer and professional artist.

Several decades ago while working in my early 20s at an accounting division job at a department store, I often walked past the doorway to my employer's advertising layout department. At the time my knowledge of mathematics remained limited, leaving me with a sense that my job was boring and unfulfilling. With budding talent in art, though, my heart yearned to draw and create images that could stir people's passions.

Each time I walked by the advertising layout department, that division impressed me as an intimidating place staffed by high-end professionals who had spent many years preparing for such careers. To this point, I lacked such experience, although many people had told me that they honestly believed my drawing abilities were nothing less than amazing.

Each time I walked past the advertising division's open door, I saw four artists working diligently to make wonderful, creative print ads. Sometimes I would stand still in the hallway, staring in awe at these sophisticated women.

Eventually as the weeks and months passed, I gradually began wondering every day about how someone like me could ever work in such a glamorous, creative environment.

During the few years immediately prior to this, I had decided to attend the widely acclaimed California College of the Arts in San Francisco.

Since my parents lacked tuition money, after graduating from high school I attended beauty school for one year in hopes of establishing an initial career—necessary to support myslf while eventually attending art school.

I never made it to art school and married instead. After getting married, I worked at a beauty shop for a short time, but disliked working on the hair of women who insisted that their bouffant styles last from week to week.

Frustrated, I soon became what the famed song from the Broadway musical "Grease" glamorizes as a "beauty school dropout." Now with a young child at home to support, I secured the boring accounting position that left me feeling discouraged and unfulfilled.

"How can I make a positive change?" I asked myself. "How can I get the position that I desperately desire, within the advertising layout department?"

My heart gave me the only logical answer, telling me that I must generate the necessary courage to ask for such a position. So, finally one day I walked into the art department.

"How can I have a chance to work in your department?" I *asked* Possie, its director, an imposing woman with bright blue eyes and a very fashionable, stunning figure.

Possie gave a no-holds-barred answer that struck me as challenging: "Patty, anyone who works here needs to have an art degree, such as the one I earned from the Art Center in Los Angeles." Although this might have seemed discouraging at least in the short-term, she also told me of an encouraging development. A short time earlier, Possie had hired a non-degreed young woman and had begun training her.

"Patty, we're in the process of hiring for another artist position, so I would like you to bring in your portfolio," Possie said.

"Sounds great, thank you," I told her, never revealing that I lacked such documentation. I worked at home through the following weekend creating precise fashion-oriented artwork, using images from magazines as models while developing my own signature style.

I gave these samples to Possie the following week. Then, during the subsequent three weeks I waited in anticipation as many hopeful applicants paraded through the layout department.

Imagine the joy I felt the day when Possie unexpectedly told me,

"Patty, you're hired." As the years progressed, this significant development opened a floodgate of positive changes in my life that would last for decades.

Within the next several years, I became art director for the California Chamber of Commerce, art director of the Nevada Department of Tourism and Economic Development, and eventually a faculty member in the department of publications and graphics while also teaching students the craft of magazine layouts.

These transitions inspired me to open my own graphics design business. Eager to get on the cutting edge of technology, in the the early 1980s I became one of the first entrepreneurs in the Western United States to use computers to generate images for major corporations such as First Interstate Bank.

Nonetheless, adding to my many career blessings, the skills I honed while at the department store later served me well in my work creating fine art portraiture for clients on a commissioned basis.

Perhaps most important, my courage in seeing Possie as a young woman put me on the path to eventually meet the man of my dreams—my husband today, Wayne Rollan Melton, the author of this book.

After I divorced the father of my two children in 1984, and after ten years of being single, I was ready for a relationship. Oh! I dated lots of fellows but nobody seemed right. Finally I wrote down on a piece of paper the qualities I wanted in a man and *asked* the creator to introduce me to this person. Many of the features required of this man included firmness, sensitivity, creativity and a desire to always learn.

In 1995, Wayne had telephoned advertising professionals, asking them to give him names of the most talented graphic designers and artists. Then, Wayne asked me and four other designers to participate in a contest, each creating unique images of the Cossette logo from the hit Broadway musical "Les Miserables."

Wayne and I met during the contest, soon to fall in love and marry. This positive path in life had all been made possible because as a young woman I generated enough courage to ask for a job that—at least on paper—I seemed unqualified to receive.

Today, Wayne and I enjoy working together to create, distribute and market his books—each using our God-given talents in hopes of helping to make the world a much better place, hopefully while enriching the lives of others.

At this juncture, what instrumental questions have you asked within your own life? Could you have asked more of other people during pivotal periods, amid life-changing events? What would have been best for you, in generating and making such queries?

The compelling life lessons that Wayne sets out in the pages that follow give energizing stories and methods of opening up your life to many positive choices. To accomplish this, as you'll soon discover, all we need to do is develop the right and perfect ways to ask—seizing each moment possible for whatever the heart desires.

—Patty Atcheson-Melton

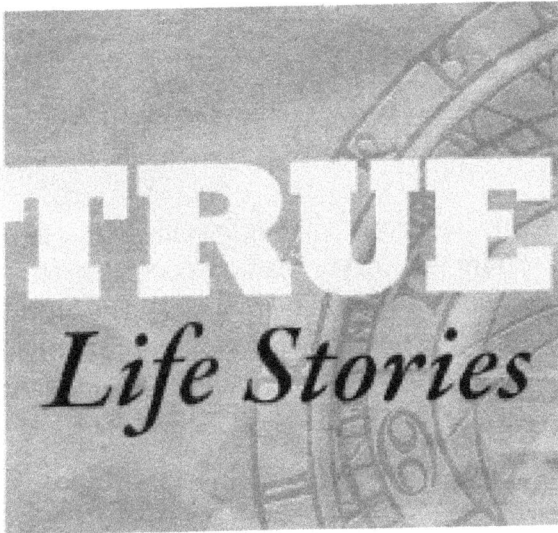

CHAPTER ONE

Conflict starts everything

"You just have to bite the bullet!"

Hearing this order from one of his acting instructors, actor Keanu Reeves gave a response that "People Magazine" reported many years later.

"Yeah, but I don't have to eat the whole rifle!" Reeves responded to the teacher.

This conflict at the Toronto School for the Performing Arts had erupted over creative differences, before administrators there booted Reeves from their institution.

Back then in the early 1980s, in his late teens, Reeves was still an unknown actor—far from a household name who commands tens of millions of dollars per film like he does today.

The Canadian setting was far from the world and lifestyle of preteen

Shia LeBeouf, barely 10 years old in the mid-1990s when he began asking his mother, Shayna, to help him find an acting agent.

According to media reports, although young Shia's mother had good intentions for him, she never made a concerted effort to help his dream come true. That might seem understandable since, after all, the boy's family reportedly had difficulty making ends meet amid their struggle for survival in a tough, down-and-out neighborhood of Los Angeles.

Just 13 years later, in the first decade of the 21st Century, Shia had joined the ranks of the movie industry's biggest superstars, commanding huge salaries per movie while in his mid-20s.

Hardship was similar or perhaps even worse way back in 1974 for the then-unknown 12-year-old Thomas Cruise Mapother IV, later known to the world as actor Tom Cruise. Media accounts insist that while a pre-teen Tom helped get food for his destitute family by delivering newspapers.

During the subsequent three decades, Cruise emerged as one of the biggest film stars the movie world had known, his movies collectively grossing billions of dollars.

Remember that everyone has a dream

Today, you have something in common with these men, although each might seem in a far different realm than you, both physically and financially.

Like Reeves, LeBeouf and Cruise, you have the ability to ask for change. You have the ability to ask for new opportunities. And you have the ability to ask for whatever you want, whenever you want as long as the right situation presents itself or you put yourself into a position to issue whatever requests you desire—no matter how outlandish they might seem. The actors mentioned so far serve as prime examples of how that happens.

Lacking the right people to ask for big acting jobs within his immediate environment while in his late teens, after getting booted from school Reeves drove many thousands of miles alone to Hollywood. There, the young man asked for and received assistance from his former father-in-law, Paul Aaron, a director of movies and Broadway plays.

Aaron gave young Reeves names of a few industry connections, and from then on this budding thespian kept asking whoever he could for acting jobs, until he found a reliable agent and his dream began coming true.

When still barely age 12, LeBeouf finally took matters into his own hands, allowing his fingers to do the walking through the Yellow Pages®. Although this might sound like a cliché, the tactic worked for the child. At least judging by media accounts, the boy literally raced through the directory, calling as many numbers as he could from listings in the "acting agents" section.

Journalists and film biographers later quoted LeBeouf as confessing that he had impersonated an adult during the phone calls, touting himself as the greatest sensation to hit Hollywood. The tactic paid off for the aspiring young actor, who promptly got an agent before going on to co-star in the Disney Channel's former "Even Stevens" series. This new exposure positioned LeBeouf to catapult to fame in films like "Holes," "I Robot," "Transformers," and "Indiana Jones & the Kingdom of the Crystal Skull."

From early childhood, Cruise had perhaps the most difficult career route of the three. After attending at least eight elementary schools in numerous cities, Cruise suffered a debilitating knee injury while on his high school wrestling team. Energetic and seeking a way to release his boundless energies, while recovering from his injury Cruise won the lead role in a "Guys and Dolls" production at his high school.

This transition began a pattern where Cruise started to ask for whatever acting roles, agents and professional associations that he wanted. While some observers might call his subsequent successes as mere good luck, others credit the characteristics of persistence and tenacity—attributes Cruise is still known for today. His many film roles range from "Taps" to blockbusters like "Jerry Maguire" and "Mission Impossible."

Needless to say, if Cruise, Reeves and LeBeouf had not mustered enough gumption to start asking as many people as possible for help, we might never have heard of any of them.

So, what about your situation? Where are you in life, and how many of your dreams have yet to come true? Like many people, perhaps you've heard about the great power of asking, of the many benefits made possible by simply inquiring about help or assistance.

Oh, sure, you've undoubtedly done plenty of asking since early childhood. Like most of us, perhaps you cried for food as a toddler, screaming at the top of your lungs in hopes of getting attention from your caregivers, most likely your parents.

Sure enough, from infancy you wanted and craved your mommy's breast or a baby bottle, and more often than not—you got them, either by looking cute, wailing your fool little head off or maybe even getting treats stuck in your mouth without asking at all.

If you hailed from a similar environment as most young Americans, by kindergarten and elementary school, you started getting told of the appropriate times and places to ask for things. Your parents probably taught you to "always say 'thank you' and 'please.'"

Depending on their own personalities or by learning from others, many young children start screaming or throwing temper tantrums in efforts to get what they want. More often than not, such attempts either result in getting the desired object or activity or—much worse—a stern lecture from an adult, a time-out in a corner, or even a butt paddling.

Looking back, at least in some ways, this process seemed natural, since after all, we've been asking for things or positions within society for as long as we remember. In fact, if you stop and think about the process a moment, as a young adult or adult, you actually ask for "things" all day long, whether you think about the process or not.

Gradually this behavior has reached a so-called autopilot or merry-go-round phase, where the media, billboards and various other forms of advertising continually ask you "to buy." This starts from the moment you awaken in the morning until you finally go to sleep.

All along, whether realizing this or not, you continually ask for things yourself. While en route to work or school, for instance, you might buy a particular amount of gas, undoubtedly sometimes after lumbering through convenience stores scouring for your favorite junk foods or perhaps after first gobbling breakfast at home.

In the consumer phase of this process, many of us ask for or seek out "objects" that we believe will meet our needs. These encompass everything from favorite toothpaste flavors to preferred brands of gum—anything we crave "right away."

Much of the time, many people strive to avoid those annoying moments when people or corporations ask us "to buy." As a result, we often zip past TV commercials with TiVo® remote controls, or find ourselves forced to watch the ads because our homes lack such convenient devices. Radio, TV, newspaper and Internet advertisements strive to grab everyone's attention, seemingly non-stop throughout the day. As if all this weren't already mind-boggling enough, seemingly everywhere people go in urban and many rural environments, signs and billboards beg for their attention. Famed analysts have proclaimed that "the media is the message," but what about you? What do you really want? Just as important, do you realize all this is happening?

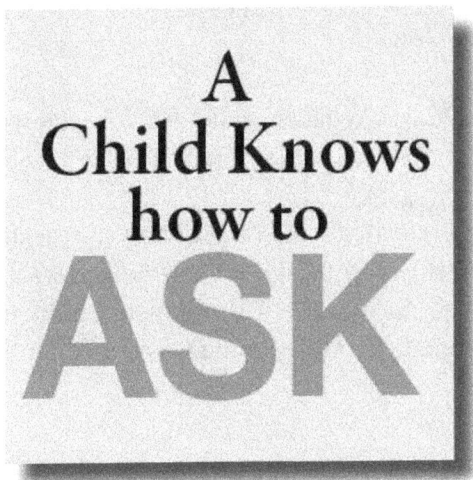

A
Child Knows
how to
ASK

CHAPTER TWO

Think about what you really want

The phrase "stop the world, I want to get off" was made famous in an early 1960s musical by that name, produced by Leslie Bricusse and the late Anthony Newly. The production's many tunes included the catchy and eternally memorable "What Kind of Fool am I," made famous worldwide thanks to a recording by the late legendary entertainer Sammy Davis Jr.

Today, many of us want to stop the world and get off, at least in a sense, largely because we're tired of just about everything and everyone asking for things. And, in a sense, lots of people think of themselves as the type of fool that's described in the tune.

The copyrighted lyrics follow the initial "what kind of fool am I" line with "who never fell in love ~ It seems that I am the only one that I have been thinking of."

Well, in this vein, perhaps now would be a good time for you to pause and think for a moment. Think about what you really want in life, what you still would like to achieve. What are your dreams, and what would make you happier than you are today, if anything?

Chances seem great that you've probably never asked for all the things that you truly want. Sure, everyone suffers at least some degree of heartache during life. But for you, could such tribulations have been lessened, if only you had asked for more of what you truly wanted?

Herein rests other vital questions: What could you ask for now that would help make your dreams become reality, or at least position your desires to be fulfilled? Would asking be pointless, a mere exercise in futility? Are you asking for enough of the "right" things, and what about your loved ones—the people you care about, relatives, friends or acquaintances? Have you been asking enough of the most appropriate questions on their behalf as well?

Thus far in life, if you have not yet taken time to slow down for awhile and ask these questions, then what is the point to your existence here anyway?

So, herein rests an ideal juncture, a place where you can reflect on these many questions, generating a pathway filled with queries that you might decide to start asking—perhaps changing your life for the better.

First off, re-learn the glorious art of asking

As a child, actor Ronald William "Ronnie" Howard—later known as "Ron"—became a household name nationwide as co-star of "The Andy Griffith Show" sitcom in the early 1960s. Portraying the beloved character Opie, son of Sheriff Andy Taylor, little Ronnie stole the hearts of people across America through the program's initial run.

The show's producers had recruited the boy following his early success in "The Music Man" movie starring Shirley Jones and Robert Preston. During his eight-year run on Griffith's show, Howard gave great movie performances in "The Courtship of Eddie's Father" with Glenn Ford, and as a guest star on other TV programs—such as an episode of "I Spy" with Bill Cosby and Robert Culp.

Although already well positioned with a solid, stable acting career, little Ronnie became widely respected within the industry. The boy's associates appreciated him for asking lots of questions, unafraid to learn from adults about what the production and direction process entailed.

Rather than putting forth queries in order to gain a career or fame, which Ronnie already had, the boy yearned for more knowledge. So, by his early teens when Griffith's show finally ended following an eight-year run in 1968, Ronnie Howard had gained knowledge on many of the basics necessary to produce and direct films and TV shows.

Later, during and after a successful six-year run on TV's hit sitcom "Happy Days" from 1974-1980, now known as Ron Howard, he began asking film industry executives a different question. This time, Howard would inquire, "Will you let me direct your movie?"

Howard's dogged persistence paid off when producers granted his requests, signing the actor to direct "Grand Theft Auto" in 1977 and "Night Shift" in 1982. Strengthened by the success of these productions, from his 30s and beyond the former child actor has emerged as one of the industry's most highly respected and successful directors; his many high-grossing films have included "Apollo 13" with Tom Hanks and "A Beautiful Mind" with Russell Crowe, and many more.

Our dreams about asking start as children

In 1960 while a 4-year-old student at the Holy Child day care center in Reno, Nev., Tom Hanks, then a future Academy Award®-winning actor, often drew rockets with his schoolmates. At the time, his father, Amos Hanks, who hailed from the family of Abraham Lincoln's mother, Nancy Hanks, worked as a chef in downtown Reno's former Mapes Hotel.

Tom Hanks lived with numerous brothers, sisters and his parents in the family's crammed small duplex on Mill Street near downtown, just four blocks from his father's workplace. Soon afterward, Tom's parents divorced.

Through his teens and into his early 20s, mostly in California, Hanks honed and strengthened his ability to ask and to recruit people who would help lead to his successful TV and movie career, including the starring role in the "Apollo 13" movie that Ron Howard directed.

For the most part, we can assume that Hanks was just like you were as a child in matters of dreams for a vibrant future. Remember, that as children, we all instinctively learned the ability to ask. Since childhood, some of us have used these skills more than others, sometimes in vastly different ways.

So, now as an adult, what changes can you ask for in your life?

Do you have the courage and gumption to make such requests?

And, perhaps most important, how would you go about issuing such queries?

Realize many questions go unanswered

While with her family hiding from the Nazis in Amsterdam in the early 1940s, a teenage Jewish girl, Anne Frank, wrote in her eventually famous diary that she hoped someday to return to school to complete her studies. Without contact with the outside world, Anne lacked the ability to ask anyone other than relatives for help or assistance.

Acting on a tip from a source that has never been revealed, the Nazi Gestapo arrested the Frank family and several of their Jewish friends in August 1944. One month later, the Nazis deported the Franks to the concentration camp at Auschwitz; seven months after that, in March 1945 Anne died at age 15 of typhus in the Bergen-Belsen concentration camp.

Like countless children throughout history, Anne never had a chance to ask anyone of great power other than her god for significant help, for freedom for herself and for her relatives. Today, she and other brave children serve as silent mentors to all the rest of us who have been blessed with ample chances to ask for better opportunities—but squandered or failed to seize the magnificent chances that our lives have presented.

Patrick Bouvier Kennedy, son of the late President John F. Kennedy and First Lady Jacqueline Kennedy, likely could have gone on to fame and possible power due to name recognition, but he died at just two days old in 1963. Pauline Robinson Bush, sister of former President George W. Bush, born three years after this future commander-in-chief, died of leukemia in 1953, barely four years old.

The seventh shogun of the Tokugawa Dynasty of Japan, Tokugawa Ietsugu, died in 1716 at age seven, well before any chance to mature and wield his power. Showing perhaps even more promise, Edward

VI of England, assumed the throne at age nine upon the death of his father, the notorious King Henry VIII. The Regency Council governed the realm from Edward's ascension until his death, possibly from lung disease, at age 15 in Greenwich near London in 1553.

The untimely deaths of these notable children send an eternal message that the power to ask sometimes remains impossible due to circumstances beyond our control. Even people lucky enough to live to extremely old age sometimes lack the ability to ask for things that matter dearly to them, in some cases due to their positions in society.

Wise beyond her years, Frank had written in her diary that "parents can only give good advice or put them on the right paths, but the final forming of a person's character lies in their own hands."

Taking a much different perspective, Clarence Darrow, a famed American lawyer who died at age 80 in 1938, once proclaimed that the first half of our lives are ruined by our parents, and the second half by our children.

To be sure, the power to ask for something significant in life—and to ask for those benefits now—comes only to those of us lucky enough to seek such opportunity, whether we're young or old or somewhere in between.

Rules of the Asking Game were passed on through the ages

Steady and strong, an old Chinese proverb holds true, that one generation plants the trees and another gets the shade.

As President Harry S. Truman once said, "I have found the best way to give advice to your children is to find out what they want and to give it to them."

With this understood, let us always remember the proclamations of those psychologists, scholars and self-help advisors who proclaim that a childlike quality, an innocence and a curiosity remains within us all—no matter how young or old.

In his classic book "All I Really Need to Know I Learned in Kindergarten," Robert Fulghum, teaches of the humor, imagination and hope that springs forth from our spirits as children, qualities that we can retain as adults.

"Your children are not your children," said Khalil Gibran, a noted theologian, writer and philosopher from Lebanon who died in New York City in 1931 at age 48. "They are the sons and daughters of life's longing for itself."

All along, throughout the process of learning what to ask for from life, and then putting those queries into action, a clear message remains that we all should enjoy life's challenges—without necessarily making each quest into a tragedy that needs to be overcome. The great American humorist Mark Twain, in his prime during the late 1800s, made this abundantly clear: "Adam and Eve had many advantages, but the principal one was that they escaped teething."

To fully grasp these many truisms, let us learn to discover our abilities to develop and seek out new questions that—individually—we might have failed to grasp, envision or appreciate in the past. Only through such innocent inner reflection can we truly take hold of those dreams that our souls want us to achieve.

As we mature enough to realize that we can be very young at heart, our responsibilities rest on our ability to make conscious choices with our serious minds or our childlike intuition.

"I don't know anything about luck," the late TV comedienne Lucille Ball, star of the 1950s smash sitcom "I Love Lucy," was once quoted as saying. "I've never banked on it, and I'm afraid of people who do. Luck to me is something else, hard work and realizing what is opportunity and what isn't."

Taking a reverse philosophy of sorts, Clarence Frank Birdseye II, an American inventor—founder of the frozen food industry, who died in 1956 at age 69—advised us to "go around asking a lot of damnfool questions and taking chances. Only through curiosity can we discover opportunities, and only by gambling can we take advantage of them."

Walt Disney learned to take gambles

Perhaps history's greatest seer into the hearts and minds of children, the legendary Walt Disney showed his genius when *asking* all the right questions in creating Disneyland and the related empire that today generates at least $35 billion in annual revenue.

During his teens, Disney made decisions that some observers might consider questionable—*asking* to join the Red Cross at age 16 in 1917. The budding young artist had recently dropped out of high school to join the army during World War I, only to be rejected because he was too young.

Because Disney *asked* to join, the Red Cross was only kind enough to oblige, sending him near the front lines in France to drive an ambulance for a one-year stint. Not long after his return to the Chicago area, Disney set out for Kansas City to launch his artistic career. There, he *asked* his brother Roy for help obtaining a job through a friend at the Pesmen-Rubin Art Studio.

Soon landing a job there, Disney kept busy generating print media advertisements that included movie theater promotions. Increasingly industrious, Disney kept asking for opportunity or, with the help and cooperation of others, he made his desires into reality.

In 1920, within a year of getting the art job, Disney and cartoonist Ubbe Iwerks formed "Iwerks-Disney Commercial Artists." Following a rough start, they soon began working at another Kansas City-based film company, where Disney developed an interest in animation and decided to become an animator.

During the course of the next few decades, Disney became an expert in *asking* for and seizing almost every available opportunity he deemed worthwhile. Always on the lookout for new or exceptional talent, he recruited another co-worker and soon started showing animated films called "Laugh-O-Grams" at local theaters.

Encouraged by the film's regional success, Disney soon *asked* for more employees to join his animation company. Undaunted after this operation went bankrupt following his difficulties managing money, Disney decided to create a studio in Hollywood, the world's film mecca.

Amid various start-ups and stops due to temporary setbacks, Disney never let up in his efforts to *ask* for financing and to *ask* for—and to lead—the development of new animated characters. The most notable included the world famous Mickey Mouse, based on a pet that Disney once had at a Kansas City studio.

A string of other notable animated Disney characters were developed through the 1930s, including Donald Duck. Perhaps largely because of Disney's childlike curiosity and boundless imagination, the company continued thriving and growing as he aged. His studio reigned supreme through the so-called Golden Age of Animation, primarily during the late-Depression era of late 1930s.

Disney's most notable creations of this era included "Snow White and the Seven Dwarfs," "Fantasia," "Pinocchio," "Bambi," and "Dumbo." Following a string of successful morale-boosting creations during the World War II period from 1940-1945, a subsequent string of hits through 1955 included "Bugs Bunny," "Cinderella," and "Alice in Wonderland."

More childlike and energetic than ever, unsatisfied to merely accept the many successes he already had achieved, beginning in the late 1940s Disney worked for five years straight to plan and build Disneyland—asking for as many resources as possible. The famed amusement facility in the Southern California community of Anaheim opened in July 1955.

We can all create with childlike abandon

Perhaps today your dreams are on a much smaller scale than Disney's. Maybe at this point, all you'd like to *ask* for is a meager pay raise or even a job, just enough so that you'll have the resources to make ends meet. Or, maybe you've put your life on a designated course, hoping for a specific type of job with a pre-designed pay schedule.

Still others embrace the so-called American dream, a house in the suburbs or a car, while generating enough income to adequately support the family.

For his part, back when many of today's middle-aged folks were still children, Disney remained on his personal quest of always **asking** for more and more. He sought whatever was possible to meet the growth requirements of his company and the needs or desires of consumers that the enterprise served.

Applauded worldwide for his visionary personality, Walt Disney was quoted as telling an associate when planning Disneyland that

"I just want it to look like nothing else in the world." Disney lived his life as a man who yearned to dream big and rarely if ever did he think on a small, limited scale.

To him, it seems, to coin the old cliché, the "sky is the limit." And so Disney kept *asking* for more from himself, from the community, from other businesses and from consumers nationwide. Perhaps most of all, he asked consumers what they wanted, and then he fulfilled their dreams—essentially making our society's healthy fantasies come true.

Following a string of other film successes including "Treasure Island," "20,000 Leagues Under the Sea," "Lady and the Tramp," and many more, in 1966 Disney—a chain smoker—died of lung cancer in Burbank, Calif., at age 65.

Much of the company's many successes also hinged on the visions and skills of its co-founder, his brother, Roy Disney, another expert in the art or skill of *asking* who died in 1971 at age 78.

All these years later, when visiting Disney entertainment facilities, watching the Disney Channel or seeing any of the many film releases that feature the company's world-famous castle image at the beginning, we can say: "This all started because of a man with a child-like vision who knew how to *ask* and then to keep *asking* for more."

In remembering Walt Disney and his many accomplishments, each of us can take heart in knowing that we all possess the same type of inner spirit and heart that he was blessed with.

The secret lies in knowing how to unlock this boundless, unlimited and positive spirit that dwells within the souls of us all. To think positive and to embrace all the good possibilities that life might offer can spark a guiding torch within our hearts.

Right now at this very moment within you rests a dream, a desire, a yearning to fulfill a quest, no matter what stage in life you're in. Whether your short-term desire ranges from living peacefully in a rest home to starting off for college, remember that you can always ask just like Walt Disney made a healthy habit of doing.

Set your sights beyond mere fantasy

Far from the world of big-name entertainment, movie superstars and business icons, the vast majority of us toil through life—away from the limelight. Most of the world's 6 billion inhabitants remain unaware that you even exist. Beginning from the minute of our births, we gradually learned what interests us most as individuals.

Out of experience, most of us learned one of the most popular words—"No." Our parents always hollered this on a seemingly daily basis, especially when we seemed to approach danger or mischievous situations that most adults prefer that children avoid.

"No," you can't play in the gutter. "No," you can't walk through the house with those muddy shoes on. And "no," you can't have that pack of candy, although you're screaming your head off at the moment like a 3-foot-tall fool, crying louder than a lonely wolf wailing at the moon as you sit in the shopping cart here beside the checkout stand.

From the start, the word "no" seemed almost so prevalent that we might have blocked it out of the mind, at least to a degree. "No," you can't stay up as late as you want at night, and "No," you've got to go to school today although you want to stay home and play.

As this journey progressed, the word "yes" seemed far less frequent, making many of us believe that any positive response was a miracle. For the most part if we learned to behave or follow rules imposed upon us, we started to accept the word "no" and to obediently obey every such command.

Much later in life, especially during our late teens and 20s, increasing numbers of people started advising us to "try to hear as many no-answers as you can, because that only means you're getting closer to a 'yes.' Unless you hear lots of 'Nos,' you're not performing your job right or seeking enough opportunities."

Paradoxically, somehow we're told to start feeling guilty if we fail to hear lots of "no" responses and deep down some people throughout society convey a message that we're supposed to feel guilty if we hear too many "yes" responses as well.

Take a moment of repose, and upon some reflection this situation comes off as being somehow quite comical and tragic at the same time.

So, don't get embarrassed at this juncture, if you're feeling somehow confused, bothered or bewildered by this apparent dilemma that many of us face today.

"The paradox of courage is that a man must be a little careless of his life, even in order to keep it," said Gilbert Keith Chesterton, an influential English author who died in 1936 at age 62 after writing more than 80 books.

"Don't ask what the world needs," said Howard Thurman, an influential African American author, civil rights activist, theologian and philosopher who died in 1981 at age 82. "Ask what makes you come alive and go do it—because what the world needs is people who come alive."

CAN-DO Motivation

CHAPTER THREE

Everyday challenges can generate motivation

Contrary to popular belief, Thomas Crapper never invented the toilet—something he still gets common credit for more than 98 years after his death. Sure, because Crapper was human, his body had the standard biological needs that each of us must undergo.

Realizing that people everywhere have similar requirements, Mister Crapper started asking lots of questions while a young man in England in the mid-1800s.

By asking people what they wanted or needed, and carefully listening to their answers he discovered the basic intricacies of human life—on a much more primary scale than the type of motivations that Walt Disney would later seek from the masses.

According to some accounts, the flush toilet had been invented as far back as 1596, possibly by Sir John Herington—a design supposedly improved upon in the late 1700s, generating the first modern line of toilets.

The legend of Mister Crapper's life goes overboard, with some observers going so far as to falsely claim that he received a knighthood and thereby earned the designation of "Sir Thomas Crapper."

If the truth be told, Crapper made integral inventions important to the functions of the modern toilet. Perhaps most notable of these is the ballcock, a mechanism essential in the filling of water tanks like those found in flush toilets.

Like other scientists or inventors, without necessarily saying this in so many words, Crapper taught us the importance of flushing out vital details by asking—not just for things to be given—but for lots of details.

Often through such discovery processes, researchers can learn essential information and thereby ferret out certain unfulfilled needs or possible ways to solve problems.

"Our greatest weakness lies in giving up," said Thomas Alva Edison, the legendary American inventor of the first commercially practical incandescent light and many other gadgets, who died in 1931 at age 84. "The most certain way to succeed is always to try just one more time."

Like the world's other great inventors, Edison always asked many questions of himself and of others, continually on the prowl for problems and solutions. Along the way to eventually generating more than 1,000 patents in his name, Edison became famous in part for his eagerness and willingness to pursue new, unique or potentially better solutions.

"Everything comes to him who hustles while he waits," said Edison, notorious for continually working and finding solutions, even when at his winter vacation home in Fort Myers, Fla.

Consider your own life as if it were a mystery

Perhaps this analogy appears dead wrong, but odds seem great that to this point in your life, you have not asked nearly as many questions as Crapper or Edison would have—about your own life, or about the environment immediately around you.

Some of us trudge through life, lumbering in any direction that activities seem to take us, without trying to set the course ourselves. People within this realm come off as either too timid to take risks, or unsure of what questions to ask, or even both.

And because it's their nature, other folks, especially those in the so-called Type-A personality set, want to buzz through every possibility, constantly on the go both personally and professionally. To hear these people talk like non-stop buzz saws can become irritating, while they jabber—primarily about their own wants and needs.

At this juncture, while pondering the many diverse possibilities that the asking process can entail, we find some of the most enticing strategies or self-discovery methods. Among them:

● **Self:** What does the heart say, the deep-deep soul, about where and how you want your life to progress? What, ultimately, would make you happiest?

● **Partner:** How does your spouse, partner or lover fit into this long-tem picture, if at all? What, if anything, would you be willing to sacrifice or do for this person?

● **Family:** Does your family fit into this picture, the long-term message that springs forth from your soul? In what ways do you want to share with them, if at all?

● **Work:** Does your chosen career give you a sense of satisfaction, or at least how much pleasure or fulfillment does your profession ignite within the spirit? Could any other line of work make you feel more vibrant and more alive, free-flowing rather than stagnant?

● **Friends:** Do you have enough friends or the "right kind" of acquaintances, at least in the sense that they're people who can enable you to grow professionally and spiritually? And if you have only a few friends or none, is that okay when it comes to your spirit?

● **Environment:** Are the places that you live and work where you want to remain for the rest of your life? Would other settings help give you a better sense of fulfillment, in matters of health and how you relate to the world?

As this self-assessment process begins, you can ask the most questions of yourself rather than seeking the advice and suggestions of others. This initial phase or step can emerge as the most important stage within the process as you expand your horizons, discovering the many possibilities that life can offer.

"This above all: to thine own self be true," says Shakespeare's Hamlet, faced with the possibility of exacting revenge against his father's killer. Einstein seemed to take a different view when he said that "To understand the world, one must not be worrying about one's self."

A self-assessment becomes necessary

Perhaps by asking questions of ourselves, as if interviewed by a fantasy news reporter, we can breeze past our own selfishness or quirky human desires. Whatever the method, the beauty here beams bright, the revelation that when asking questions of yourself and eventually of others, you reign as the master of your own universe. You're the king or queen, the only person who decides what questions to put forth.

"Trust yourself," advised the late Benjamin Spock, M.D., a widely acclaimed American pediatrician and author of "Baby and Child Care," a runaway bestseller from the mid-1900s, well into the 1970s and beyond. "You know more than you think you do."

From the start, deep down rests the initial questions—and ultimately the answers—that you'll generate for yourself. Take comfort in knowing that at least through this initial stage, no one but you needs to know that you're engaged in self-discovery.

"Man is least himself when he talks in his own person," said Oscar Wilde, an Irish playwright and poet who died in 1900 at age 46. "Give him a mask and he will tell you the truth."

Within the corridors of these various assessments, only you can take the essential steps necessary to undergo this initial self-discovery process. To avoid such a crossroads would only serve to put you onto a needless track, for you're the best person to determine the course and strategy of how and when to ask for things integral to your life.

Aristotle, the Greek philosopher who lived to age 62 more than 300 years before Christ, places the burden in this regard squarely on your shoulders: "Happiness belongs to the self-sufficient."

Asking questions can take courage

As this journey begins, you'll need to know that asking questions— both of yourself and of others—can seem daunting, difficult or even dangerous. Especially for those unused to making such queries, the mere thought can bring shivers to the spine.

While pondering these possibilities, consider the classic "Cinderella" story. Both the original French and German versions of this world-famous fairy tale portray Cinderella as a sweet, soft and loving young woman harassed by a wicked, selfish lady—possibly a stepmother, depending on which version is considered from various eras and regions of the world.

In many versions, the stepmother and her equally vain daughters— Cinderella's stepsisters—force her to toil at grueling housework. Yet in none of the most prevalent versions do we hear Cinderella asking to be set free, asking them why they're cruel, or asking her own father to free her from such slavery.

Only a handsome prince emerges as able to save Cinderella; he marries this beautiful young woman and whisks her off to his castle. The moral persists that beauty prevails, while the ability to remain gracious remains another priceless quality.

Now in the real-world setting of this moment, though, who serves as your handsome prince or beautiful princess? Of course, from the standpoint of learning to ask the right questions, the answer for you emerges: "Me, myself, and I."

Learn about asking from a popular fairy tale

Understandably, in a sense, you're more powerful than poor Cinderella during the days before she met the handsome prince. Unlike she did, you can ask the necessary questions to free yourself into a world of happiness, even if a blunt, direct strategy becomes required.

Through innocence and grace we can find a natural path, the best course for each of us. Since our lives are not pre-scripted such as Cinderella's, we can and should utter necessary questions to set ourselves free from bondage.

At this moment, deep down you might feel enslaved or captured, not by a wicked stepmother but by something even worse than that. You might feel discouraged, ultimately by your previous failure to ask the right questions—an oversight that resulted in decisions that got you where you are today, at this very moment.

When initially dating your current spouse or lover, did you show courage needed to ask the right questions of that person? Did you ask about lifestyle choices that you might have sharply disagreed with? Or, did you take the safe route, preferring to avoid having to hear potential answers that might have set your life on a different course?

Just as daunting, did you ask enough of the right questions when accepting a job with your current employer—that is, if you're lucky enough to have work? Did you merely accept the position right away without mustering enough courage to ask about integral policies, only to find yourself now unhappy because you failed to ask—ultimately discovering that today you work under employment policies that you consider repulsive, offensive or disrespectful?

Well, if some or all this holds true for you now, take solace in knowing that, with luck or the type of persistence that Thomas Edison embraced, you can begin asking the right questions to suit your situation.

Consider the story in the hit 1993 movie "Sleepless in Seattle," starring Tom Hanks as Sam Baldwin and Ross Malinger as his son Jonah Baldwin. Without showing any apparent nervousness, Jonah asks Annie Reed, played by Meg Ryan, to meet them at the top of the Empire State Building.

Following some initial tension and logistical confusion, in the end they all meet up at the designated site—opening the possibility of happiness, all because this boy had either the courage or the innocence necessary to ask.

Muster up necessary emotional strength

Has anyone ever asked you to marry him or her, or perhaps the other way around? Drama results, since beforehand the question always poses itself, that the object of affection and love might actually say "No."

Like it or not, the perennial hit ABC-TV reality show "The Bachelor," which entered its 13th season at the beginning of 2009, remained popular largely for this very reason.

As humans, we instinctively know that in order to achieve our dreams in life, we're required to ask potentially risky questions like: "Can I have this job?" or "Can we move to a different town?" or even "Will you marry me?"

Tens of millions of Americans get magnetized by personal drama, either in their own lives or on TV shows such as this. Some men undoubtedly laugh or playfully pester their wives or girlfriends who insist on watching the program.

Many viewers admit to a sense of drama, especially at the end of each episode when the lucky bachelor individually asks specific women that he prefers to remain on the show for subsequent episodes. Any women that the bachelor decides not to ask essentially get dumped, and those that he asks to stay also have the option of rejecting his proposals.

Some viewers laugh or cry during the final minutes of each program, especially during each season's last episode when the bachelor rejects one woman—while invariably asking the only remaining finalist to marry him.

Most often in the final episode the last woman to get rejected is shown wailing, unable to hold back tears because she loved him so much. Most of these discarded gals end up saying things like: "It's going to be so hard to get over this."

Just as predictable, the chosen woman usually ends up crying when the bachelor pulls out a wedding ring and asks the big question. All this might sound super-silly to some potential viewers, but the program reigns as mighty serious to those who help keep the ratings relatively solid.

Maybe people watch this show in part because the real-live reality characters have to undergo what each of us must endure during the course of our lives. Like those people on the screen, we face rejection and heartache. And like them, we're probably going to hear plenty of "no" answers or flat-out rejections to the many questions we must present.

Is there really a sucker born every minute?

A parade of characters performed in "The Gong Show," a mid-1970s TV game program starring host Chuck Barris. By performing, the contestants essentially were asking the world—or more specifically the show's judges—to accept them.

Much of the time, one or more of the judges bolted up from their seats, took hold of a large stick and smashed it against a gong or giant drum. This signaled the end or demise of the contestant, summarily stopped from performing.

Odd as this might sound, in real life each of us faces the possibility of being gonged every day, and in fact we started getting rejected by our teachers and by some of our classmates from pre-school onward. Instructors issued gongs by imposing less-than-perfect grades, and some classmates rejected us by refusing admission into their cliques.

Collectively as a society, we're essentially banging the gong against TV shows that ask us to like them. Invariably, we eventually refuse the requests to watch, resulting in cancellations, despite promo commercials that had promised the world that this would be an exciting show. The more power we have to accept or reject others, the greater we feel — at least many of us do anyway.

Consider for instance the hit FOX-TV show "American Idol," often television's highest-rated program drawing tens of millions of viewers. At the start of each season, literally thousands of singers seek to perform as contestants — essentially asking viewers and the judges to like and approve their entertainment.

Eager for their big dreams of stardom to come true, tens of thousands end up getting rejected. Within the first several episodes, the judges whittle the number of contestants down to a few dozen or so. That total gets cut in half within a few weeks, leaving a dozen.

Certainly, some viewers must relish the pain and heartache the rejected contestants have to endure, just as much as audiences like seeing each week's victors celebrate — because they have survived to compete in a subsequent episode.

Finally, late each May the ultimate winner, the year's "American Idol" gets chosen, guaranteed a major recording contract. All these step-by-step details get mentioned here because essentially through life each of us must endure rejection, emotional pain and heartache after we ask for acceptance — only to get rejected.

And while Americans ultimately like and gravitate toward people they perceive as "winners," each year's ultimate American Idol can give himself or herself a large degree of credit.

Every "American Idol" victor never would have succeeded unless that person had asked in the first place to be included on the program.

So, what course will you take, when it comes to your own decision to ask?

Will you have the courage necessary to pursue your dreams, in the face of possible rejection?

Consider the happiness quotient

According to news reports, the collective level of happiness among Americans reached a low for the year of 2008 on Dec. 11 of that year, with only 35 percent of people surveyed reporting that they were happy with life. Just 14 days later, on Dec. 25, as is customary for the Christmas holiday, the day's polls on that same question showed happiness for the year peaked on the holiday at 65 percent.

Surely, we're only as happy as we want to be, or the way that our minds tell us to react as conditions evolve—often letting our psyches know that everything is OK. With frequency, our emotions get dictated by whatever we choose to ask ourselves at any given moment.

As 2009 began, just more than two thirds of the people surveyed in Hong Kong expected the New Year to be even worse than the last, according to the "China Morning Post."

A Gallup Poll concluded that nearly eight out of ten Americans gave negative impressions of economic conditions. To many observers, such public sentiment mirrored the tone of news reports about widespread job losses.

Keeping such factors in mind, anyone beginning a self-evaluation process might consider asking himself: "How do I feel about life in general? Am I prone to severe mood swings, especially amid trying conditions such as a rough economy?"

Within these queries rests the revelation that the decision of what to ask for from life can go far beyond what to inquire of others. This extends to what to ask of ourselves about how we're deciding to react and to feel in response to local, national and international events. With so many variables involved, our minds can wander off target to the point we're unable to decide what to request, if anything.

"The optimist lives on the peninsula of infinite possibilities," said William Arthur Ward, a writer of inspirational maxims who died in 1994 at age 83. "The pessimist is stranded on the island of perpetual indecision."

Taking such philosophy as a call to action, we can and should remain vigilant in always asking ourselves for ways of achieving positive possibilities. By doing otherwise we would essentially resign ourselves to defeat, greeting the worst possible outcomes with open arms. Such a failure to ask for a greater good would signal almost certain gloom, both in spirit and in character.

"A pessimist sees the difficulty in every opportunity," said former British Prime Minister Winston Churchill, who died in 1965 at age 90. "An optimist sees the opportunity in every difficulty."

CHAPTER FOUR

Rejoice in the power of asking

Those in the Christian faith often take comfort in the biblical quote, in varying forms depending on interpretations, that essentially says: "Ask and you will receive, and your joy will be complete," from the 16th Chapter of the Book of John.

According to a saying attributed to the great spiritual master, the Buddha, "all that we are is the result of what we have thought." From the perspective of the Maharishi Yogi, a spiritual leader famous through the final half of the 20th Century, "There is nothing difficult, there is nothing complicated, only one has to have a desire to have a better quality of life."

Whatever your spiritual faith, if any, realize that what you believe can and ultimately will play a major role in the development of questions you decide to ask of yourself and of others.

Copyrighted lyrics from the hit Broadway and movie musical "The Sound of Music" urge us to "climb every mountain, search high and low, follow every byway, every path you know." Those of us who embrace such inspirational thought instinctively know what questions to ask of ourselves and of others, often in ideal times and places.

Before making his final decision to run for president, Barack Obama asked his wife Michelle for her guidance and input. The answer for both of them became "yes" after much thought and interactive discussion.

Conversely, notable public figures such as the late famed crooner Frank Sinatra, who died in 1998 at age 82, prepared for a visit to his Palm Springs, Calif., home from then-President John F. Kennedy, without first getting a definite "yes" answer. Before starting a remodeling project on his own house in anticipation of the visit, Sinatra had failed to ask or re-confirm with Kennedy directly if the visit would occur.

Finally, Kennedy decided not to attend, largely at the urging of FBI Director J. Edgar Hoover for reasons of keeping politically sensitive personal secrets. The president's brother-in-law, Peter Lawford, got the unenviable duty of informing Sinatra. Hearing the news, the entertainer went into a tirade and personally destroyed much of the remodeling project.

The lesson here remains solid and clear for those of us comparing transitions like those that faced Obama and Sinatra. Asking specific questions beforehand can ward off potential misunderstandings, nipping potential conflict in the bud.

"Shallow misunderstandings from people of good will is more frustrating than absolute misunderstanding from people of ill will," said the Rev. Dr. Martin Luther King Jr., the legendary civil rights activist slain by an assassin in 1968 at age 39.

Life's limitless possibilities come to mind upon such reflection, the notion that amid conflict we can and should ask as many questions as possible. Even from the mouths of babes, they say, great and wondrous words of wisdom can spring forth. Upon reactions such as these, particularly from those within the older generation, let's attempt to seize the best of all possibilities—eager to ask for what should rightfully be ours.

Kennedy's brother, Sen. Robert Francis "Bobby" Kennedy of New York, killed by an assassin in 1968 at age 42, retooling a phrase originally penned by George Bernard Shaw, gave perhaps his most famous statement when proclaiming: "Some people see things as they are and ask, 'Why?' I dream of things that never were and ask, 'Why not?'"

At this very moment, you can embrace such fortitude, comforted by a revelation that people much wiser and perhaps even more battle-tested have gone before us. The lessons they taught, coupled with words of wisdom, enable us to conclude that the ability to ask has been and should remain an integral part of our make-up.

Some questions are asked with evil intentions

"Turn this plane around, and take me to Cuba."

Numerous hijackers of U.S. commercial airlines made such statements, taking the law into their own hands during the 1960s and 1970s before the pattern gradually faded.

Through time immemorial for as long as people have existed, evil-doers have asked for and received the booty of ill-gotten gain.

"Give me the dough, or I'll blow your stupid head off!" became a common type of statement, uttered by actors portraying Old West bandits in many western movies and TV shows that peaked as an overall entertainment form in the 1950s, 1960s and early 1970s. Sadly, millions of people throughout history have obeyed the questions or commands of selfish tyrannical leaders in many dynasties. Responding to the requests of dictators, people from numerous cultures have inflicted vicious, widespread crimes against humanity, wiping out entire populations—from the Holocaust that killed millions of Jews in Adolph Hitler's Nazi Germany in the 1930s and 1940s, to Idi Amin's tyranny in Uganda in the 1970s.

To this end, we should know that asking is not always good. And just as depressing, responding in the affirmative to horrific requests proves heartless and sinful.

While an old-saying dictates that "to the victor goes the spoils," in reality these savage dictators and countless others through history have always gone down in flames—hopefully to hell where they belong.

"A dictator must fool all the people all the time and there's only one way to do that: he also must fool himself," said William Somerset Maugham, an English short story writer, novelist and playwright who died in 1965 at age 91.

While many millions or perhaps even billions of people yearn for a leader who'll ask or tell them what to do, those of us who aspire to sensibility vow to remain thoughtful and loving in our personal quests to ask questions of the world. Collectively and individually, we prefer a path of love, kindness, understanding, cooperation and selfless charity.

In the United States, "the remarkable thing is that we really love our neighbor as ourselves," said Eric Hoffer, a philosopher and social writer who died in 1983 at age 80, three months after receiving a Presidential Medal of Freedom from President Ronald Reagan. "We do unto others as we do unto ourselves."

Indeed, "we hate others when we hate ourselves," Hoffer said. "We are tolerant toward others when we tolerate ourselves. We forgive others when we forgive ourselves. We are prone to sacrifice others when we are ready to sacrifice ourselves."

Develop inspirational, life-changing questions

Wouldn't you love to kiss the Blarney Stone?

Perhaps you've heard of this famed bluestone, embossed in the Blarney Castle near the community of Cork in Ireland. Anyone lucky enough to kiss this stone is said to become blessed with the gift of gab.

Yes, wouldn't it be great to have the ideal, most-perfect questions to ask spring forth from your heart, seemingly with little or no effort on your part?

Of course, you could spend the thousands of dollars required for a plane trip or boat ride to Ireland, just enough in transportation costs necessary to press your lips to the stone. But then, would the trek prove worthwhile following all that effort?

For many of us, the best or more sensible solution rests within our hearts at this very moment. To be sure, within each of us sits an even more valuable stone, the core of our individual and personal convictions.

The leprechauns of Irish mythology, male faeries, would beg to differ in this regard. Undoubtedly they'd urge us to pump cash into the Irish economy, enough of our own dough to fill any available pot at the end of a rainbow.

Out of such fantasies or possibilities, an ultimate answer springs forth. The secret to developing the right questions rests within our own imaginations.

From the start, for insights into what you truly believe perhaps you'll find significant clues from the questions you want to ask in the first place. Nancy Willard, a children's book author born in Michigan in 1936, has been quoted as saying that, after all, "sometimes questions are more important than answers."

Indeed, "logic will get you from A to B," Albert Einstein said. "Imagination will take you everywhere."

Take inspiration from your heart

Inspired by all these many possibilities, we can blast off into a sensible, well-planned orbit while always on the lookout for chances to seize opportunity from the proverbial landscape below. As if seasoned astronauts, those of us launching into a quest to begin asking others can prepare beforehand for these proverbial journeys.

Our bodies, minds and spirits serve as the spaceship, as the final countdown begins toward the launching of our quest. Just like NASA team members, we can and should train beforehand, only in our case in a much different sense.

"I'm just preparing my impromptu remarks," quipped Winston Churchill, the former British prime minister. Actors are trained to relax as much as possible to the point where they lose any notion of themselves, in order to give the best performances.

Like seasoned thespians, we can and should put ourselves at ease banishing any worries from our minds when delving into the great, wide world of asking others.

"A leader or a man of action in crisis almost always acts subconsciously and then thinks of the reasons for his action," said Jawaharlal Nehru, the first prime minister of India, who died in 1964 at age 74.

Indeed, "all great men are gifted with intuition," said Alexis Carrel, a French Nobel Prize winner, biologist, eugenicist and surgeon who died in 1944 at age 71. "They know without reasoning or analysis, what they need to know."

Within the motivation and spirit of such revelations, become relaxed, at ease in your mind and body. Breathe deeply, knowing all the while you're fully in control, as your naturally given inner senses order you to take the right and correct path.

"The moment of truth, the sudden emergence of a new insight, is an act of intuition," said Arthur Koestler, a widely acclaimed Jewish-Hungarian polymath author who died in 1983 at age 77. "Such intuitions give the appearance of miraculous flushes, or short circuits of reasoning.

"In fact, they may be linked to an immense chain, of which only the beginning and the end are visible above the surface of consciousness," Koestler said. "The diver vanishes at one end of the chain and comes up at the other end, guided by invisible links."

Enter the starting gate for your quest to begin asking

Unless you hail as a major celebrity or a highly recognized person within your industry, many people might view your tactics as those of an underdog. Theoretically, you're almost like the famed stallion racehorse Seabiscuit, entered into a one-on-one, two-horse race in November 1938 to determine the world championship.

In this fantasy match, your competitor—War Admiral—considered by many as the fastest horse in the universe, represents those big-name celebrities or people with power capable of getting almost any career advancement or salary they ask for.

Like Seabiscuit, because you've been considered average while making mistakes in the past, in a sense you walk with a duck wad-dle, you've got a one-eyed jockey and a nearly mute trainer. When entering the starting gate, you know that the finish line features the fulfillment of your dreams in life, the things you must ask for in order to achieve your quest for happiness.

Although somewhat experienced in the art of asking for things, you fidget nervously while side-by-side with War Admiral at the starting line.

Then, pow!

You're off in a flash the second the bell rings. Your legs represent your ability to ask, as quickly, steadily and naturally as possible. Relaxed while letting your natural skills take hold, you initially pull out ahead around the first curve.

At least within your mind, tens of thousands of excited fans scream in ecstasy. This makes you proud and provides motivation, since after all this is your life and you've only got one of them to live.

Powerful and sturdy thanks to its many connections and widespread name recognition, your opponent zips forward while cutting into your initial lead—his hooves well adjusted, those nostrils flaring with every breath. You each want many of the same things including success, a superior level of prize money or even a satisfactory mate to impress.

You give an unfazed, unworried reaction when War Admiral finally pulls neck-a-neck, your quest to ask the world for things you want still clicking at full gear.

Rather than worry about being overtaken at this point, just like the horse Seabiscuit did during that still world-famous race, you seize this opportunity to pull ahead once and for all. In record time you zip past the finish line at least four lengths ahead of your rival.

Of course, this has only been a fantasy race, a product of our imagination. Yet in so called real life, you can and will achieve many of your dreams in the weeks, months and days ahead by regularly implementing the lessons you're about to learn here.

Same old
Nothing
RESULTS

CHAPTER FIVE

Get ready to jump stumbling blocks

At this point in the fantasy training process, keep in mind that plenty of stumbling blocks lay strewn across the competition track ahead. Usually the primary obstacles involve financial setbacks, substance abuse, a lack of faith, nay-sayers who continually tell you that your dreams seem unrealistic, difficulties with time management, and inadequate willpower.

Especially amid rough economic periods, extreme or persistent financial hardships can leave many people feeling they lack adequate resources to ask for what they need or want. A severe economic recession that hit late in the first decade of this century served as a key example. Many jobless people gave up hope of ever finding employment.

Conveying a strong message for us all, famed actor Will Smith delivered a superior performance depicting a homeless man, Chris Gardner, in the 2006 movie "The Pursuit of Happyness." The story chronicles the real-life saga of Gardner, based on a best-selling book by the same name as the film.

Gardner became homeless in San Francisco amid an earlier recession in 1981 after his bone-density scanner franchise business went flat. Although lacking income and penniless, this African American entrepreneur landed a coveted unpaid internship at a major stock brokerage firm without telling the company of his severe financial predicament.

While many of us might have quit in a similar situation, Gardner mustered up the courage necessary to ask for this golden opportunity. Without any salary and lacking money for scanners that he could sell, Gardner became homeless with Christopher, his young son portrayed in the film by Smith's son, Jaden.

Gardner prevailed through this extremely difficult period of personal financial hardship, largely because he asked for many things, including: the brokerage's boss for an opportunity; the pastor of Glide Memorial Church for a place to stay rather than sleeping in subway restrooms or riding in buses all night; and of himself, to generate courage necessary to prevail.

Keep asking, no matter how poor you become

"Brother, can you spare a dime?" became a catch-phrase during the Great Depression of the 1930s, when millions of people lost their jobs. The country's financial condition worsened again at the end of the first decade of this century, as millions of people had their homes foreclosed upon and lots of consumers began losing hope.

Using any available resource at their disposal, while authorities prepared for the inauguration of President Barack Obama in January

2009, streams of homeless people converged at major public venues to ask for handouts.

Lacking food, shelter and any income sources, many of these newly homeless used their instinctive ability to ask, in order to help improve chances for their own survival. Those who let pride prevent them from asking often ended up hungry, some sleeping under bridges or in public parks.

Meantime, lots of the homeless with the gumption to ask stood still at the exits or entrances of shopping malls, while holding cardboard signs embossed with phrases such as: "Homeless. Need food. Need money. Please help now."

Depending on vagrancy laws within specific communities and the ability or willingness of police to arrest panhandlers, some of these homeless people persisted thanks to the kindness of strangers. For lots of down-and-out people with the courage to ask, a few dollars provided just enough food money to survive for another day.

Here within the richest nation on earth, in many regards the wealthiest among the homeless became those with the ability and willingness to ask. In fact, the more people that an individual destitute person asks for help on a daily basis, the greater his chances of gathering contributions.

"We sometimes think that poverty is only being hungry, naked and homeless," said Mother Teresa of Calcutta, who died in 1997 at age 87. "The poverty of being unwanted, unloved and uncared for is the greatest poverty."

Like it or not, the ability to prevail among the homeless often comes down to whom among them has the ability, courage and willingness to ask for help. A key factor often involves vital assistance from those of us with incomes or financial resources.

As a society, in small groups or in major organizations, we can embrace the old saying that "you make a living by what you get, but you make a life by what you give."

With little or no warning, many of us now in safe places or with all the so-called comforts of home could find ourselves homeless or starving as well. Take heed in knowing whatever the circumstances that kindness and having the courage to ask can mix in harmony.

One of President Abraham Lincoln's most famous statements seems appropriate in this regard: "With malice toward none, with charity for all, with firmness in the right as God gives us to see the right, let us finish the work we are in."

Overcome drug addictions in order to ask

Alcoholism or drug addiction might seem like formidable stumbling blocks along the so-called raceway toward happiness, potentially curtailing the abilities of such people to ask for help or assistance. Much of society views such attributes as even more of a stigma than homelessness and poverty.

Many of the world's most famous writers suffered from alcoholism, seemingly enough names to fill a phone book. Some of the most notable include the late Hunter Thompson, Tennessee Williams, Dylan Thomas, Dorothy Parker, Edgar Allen Poe, Truman Capote, William Faulkner, F. Scott Fitzgerald, James Joyce and Ernest Hemingway.

Despite their persistent problems with booze, each of these highly praised writers possessed the courage or instinct to ask for help from publishers, at least from the start of their illustrious careers.

In other cases, mega-famous people got sucked into the whirlpool of narcotics addictions, most notably 1950s sex goddess and movie star Marilyn Monroe—found dead in her Bentwood, Calif., home at age 36 in 1962 of an apparent drug overdose. Fans and analysts have sharp disagreements over whether Monroe had asked for adequate assistance, in any effort to recover from her addictions.

Other top-name celebrities through the period thrived amid their wild antics involving alcohol, most notably members of the notorious Rat Pack, led by free-boozing Frank Sinatra. En masse, this crooner and cohorts Sammy Davis Jr., Dean Martin, Joey Bishop and Peter Lawford hit the showroom stages of Las Vegas together and individually in the 1960s, making comedy out of their alcohol-related escapades.

At the time, none of these superstars were reported as publicly or privately asking for help or assistance in overcoming apparent alcohol problems. Lawford's many years of boozing and drug addictions hit the public limelight when he succumbed to cardiac arrest in 1984 at age 61, following health complications including liver and kidney disease.

Would Sinatra, Davis, Lawford and Martin have lived longer, more vibrant lives, if any or all of them had sought help kicking the habit of booze and cigarettes?

During the 1990s and early this century, Robert Downey Jr. became perhaps the most famous film star to confront his problems with drugs including alcohol. Police arrested Downey several times on narcotics-related charges from 1996-2001, while he unsuccessfully went through various treatment programs.

On a 2004 "Oprah" show, Downey said that after his last arrest in 2001, "I finally said, 'You know what? I don't think I can continue doing this.'" From that point Downey asked for help, sticking with his efforts to stay clean.

Admit when you need to ask for help

Only by admitting he suffered a problem and subsequently asking for assistance was Downey able to put his life back on track. Since then, he has starred in numerous hit films, including the 2008 blockbuster "Iron Man."

The long list of celebrity addiction problems gets mentioned here, since many of us know of these individuals while relating to their personal problems. Of course, the vast majority of people suffering from alcohol and drug addiction are regular folks lacking celebrity status. For them, the ability and need to start asking questions remains pivotal.

In 12-step programs embraced by Alcoholics Anonymous and numerous other recovery organizations, people suffering from addictions learn the importance of asking questions of themselves, God and others. Specific topics include a moral inventory, the willingness to make amends, and humbly asking the creator to remove our shortcomings.

Nicolas Cage and Elisabeth Shue starred in the 1995 movie "Leaving Las Vegas," where his character strives to drink himself to death — rather than asking for help. Cage won the Academy Award® as best actor for his role as Ben Anderson. Like the primary character portrayed in the film, only by seeking out help can many alcoholics begin managing their addiction to the point they can avoid the bottle.

The 1962 Blake Edwards film "Days of Wine and Roses," starring Jack Lemmon and Lee Remick, depicts how regular folks get mired into alcoholism's subtle, insidious quagmire. Working on this movie became so pivotal in the personal lives of Lemmon and Remick that years after filming wrapped, each asked for and received help in a 12-step program.

"Oh God, that men should put an enemy in their mouths to steal away their brains," wrote Shakespeare, the world's most famous playwright who died in 1616, reportedly at age 52. "That we should with joy, pleasure, revel, and applause transform ourselves into beasts!"

People suffering from such addictions can benefit from an enriched, focused program of asking for better things in life—by first conducting an inner inventory of themselves. Only then, experts say, can these people implement specific recovery steps, positioning themselves for self-enrichment in many aspects of their lives.

Although being humorous, the famed boozer and comic movie star W.C. Fields—who died in 1946 at age 66—hit the mark in this regard when stating, "I drink therefore I am."

Fulton John Sheen, former auxiliary bishop of the Archdiocese of New York, who died in 1979 at age 84, summed up such situations when proclaiming that "love is a mutual self-giving which ends in self-recovery."

According to some people who embrace 12-step programs, the path toward recovery cannot begin in earnest until we forgive ourselves for the wrongs we've caused others.

"Without forgiveness there is no future," said Desmond Tutu, the famed South African cleric. His insights hold significance to addicted individuals who are eager or motivated to put their lives into a positive phase.

By facing their addictions head on, such people stand at a vital crossroads, where all life's positive possibilities seem boundless and unlimited in potential. Getting there starts with the initial asking phase, followed by an ability to embrace an inner instinct that can help guide each of us onto a perfect path.

"The tragedy of life doesn't lie in not reaching your goal," said Benjamin E. Mays, a clergyman and American educator who died in 1984 at about age 89. "The tragedy lies in having no goal to reach. It isn't a calamity to die with dreams unfilled, but it is a calamity not to dream."

Other people will get in your way

Complicating our Asking Game competition field or raceway, another potential formidable obstacle sits within our path. Besides poverty and drug addiction, other people invariably work hard in boundless efforts to keep us discouraged—as if they want to prevent us from asking the vital questions that we need to ask in order to thrive.

Parents sometimes discourage their teenage or young adult children, occasionally saying—either openly or inadvertently—that "you cannot do that. What makes you think you can do that type of thing?"

As a prime example, consider the imaginary case of Bernadette of Sarasota, Fla, a 15-year-old ballerina who in the mid-1970s got an offer to accept a full-ride scholarship to the Julliard School in New York City, thanks to her exceptional on-stage talent.

"A career in entertainment can only lead to starvation; you don't want to accept that," said Bernadette's well-to-do father, Benjamin, who refused to help with additional necessary expenses such as transportation, food and lodging.

Lacking the courage, know-how or gumption to ask others for assistance, or even the ability to make this transition on her own, Bernadette stayed in her family's Sunshine State community. There, she concentrated on other potential career goals that all left her heart less motivated, less inspired and less fulfilled.

Even as adults, motivated people often hear negative comments from relatives, friends, associates or acquaintances. Oliver, a finance industry executive from Spokane, Wash., in his mid-40s, got pestered by his parents as he asked for and sought more development in his successful career.

Despite what many people considered his unexpected success, Oliver's folks continually complained that they failed to understand what he was doing.

Just as distressing, Pauline, a 34-year-old businesswoman in London, served as an advisor to the operator of several gold mines. Pauline continually asked many questions of people throughout the mining industry, as she strived to learn as much as she could about the precious metals business.

At breakfast during this period, Pauline advised her mother, Mabel, to buy as much gold as possible—a hedge against a possible stock market downturn. "What the hell do you know about stocks and gold!" Pauline's mother hollered, while the two ate breakfast at a restaurant. Subsequently, Mabel lost almost her entire financial fortune in the stock market downturn of 2008. The mother would have retained her fortune, had she heeded her daughter's advice.

Sure enough, as you expand and improve your own Asking Game, people you know—maybe even a lot of them—are going to do everything possible to pull the carpet out from under you. Their motivations vary through a wide spectrum ranging from plain old jealousy and greed, or even simple-minded "relatives from hell," bogged down by their own negative personalities.

While developing your dream list, creating an inventory of things that you'll eventually ask for, keep in mind that some people will strive with all their might to get in your way or to scuttle your plans.

Knowing this, how do you think you'll deal with them? What'll be the best methods for you to derail their sniveling, goofy or mindless efforts to shatter your dreams? And how can you begin or continue asking for things necessary to achieve these goals amid such unnecessary hubbub?

Always remember to stay the course

For thousands of years warriors have used the term "stay the course" in everything from minor conflicts to major battles. Commanders came to believe that victory always remained possible as long as fighters relentlessly moved toward their objective, usually no matter what the cost in finances and in blood. Later, President Ronald Reagan popularized the term during his administration from 1981-1989.

Reagan's Republican allies also began using the term "cut and run" when describing the wishes of their political rivals, primarily the Democrats. The president's supporters used this "cut-and-run" term to portray their political opponents as wimpy and cowardly, unwilling to persevere through the "stay the course" battles deemed necessary to achieve major objectives.

Embracing such philosophy, whatever your political bent, adopting a "stay the course" strategy might prove beneficial as relatives or friends strive to stop or prevent you from pursuing your admirable goals. This way, tune them out, and then keep asking the world for the things that you desire.

"Oh, are you trying to call Hollywood producers again?" a wife might say, whining at her optimistic husband as he strives to make his first appearance in the movies. "Robert, face it, no one is ever going to call you back. Heck, you're already 36 years old; you're too old to begin such a career."

Hearing such negative comments, no matter what your primary goal, should only serve to make you "stay the course" even more. Does this relative or friend bother you at home, always close to your physical environment so that he or she can butt in when least desired? Do you have a private place, away from earshot?

While remaining determined to stay the course, your primary options are to confront the person by telling him or her that you'll continue your efforts no matter what—or you can undergo your Asking Game in a clandestine manner, so that the person never knows.

Learn to persevere despite adversity

"Watson, come here, I want to see you."

Those eight words marked the first time someone had spoken via telephone, uttered by the inventor Alexander Graham Bell.

This resounding success just four days after Bell's 29th birthday in 1876 changed the world forever, thanks largely to his ability to ask many people for funding and assistance. Unlike many of us, Bell, a native of Scotland who died in Canada in 1922 at age 72, had parents who strongly encouraged him to pursue his work since childhood.

Imagine how different the world would be today, if the telephone had not yet been invented in the late 1800s and early 1900s. Firm support and encouragement from relatives can go a long way to putting teens and young adults on track toward exciting advances in technology.

Far more than mere encouragement, however, those who achieve such resounding success invariably possess a keen ability, the strength to ask others for help. Backed by his supporting parents, Bell made a habit of asking, a pattern that started during early childhood when he already displayed natural curiosity. Among these many milestones:

● **Turn negatives into positives:** The parent of a childhood buddy admonished young Bell and his pal, reportedly by asking the boys: "Why don't you do something useful?" The man suggested the lads complete the laborious task of taking husks off wheat at a mill. At age 12, Bell *asked* himself how to find an efficient solution, and he soon created a simple machine to handle the chore.

● **Inspired curiosity:** Following a spotty record in the classroom, Bell dropped out of school at age 15 and began living in London with his grandfather, Alexander Bell. There, the teenager started *asking* lots of questions, sparking a lifelong passion for learning.

● **Showed passion:** Just one year after dropping from school, the younger Bell became a pupil-teacher at Weston House Academy's music and elocution classes. Bell's keen ability to *ask* lots of questions quickly fueled his knowledge of sound, his key interest.

● **Positive publicity:** Eager to introduce the telephone to scientists, Bell managed to grab world headlines one day after *asking* his peers to see the invention in Philadelphia at the 1876 Centenary Exhibition.

Sadly, many of us lack the support system of family and friends like those who encouraged Bell. Even when without such essential backing, those of us eager to bring our queries to the world can take a variety of strategies, all of them ethical or widely accepted:

● **Deception:** When dealing with whiny, negative-minded relatives, consider using a battle-tested strategy suggested more than 400 years before Christ by Sun Tzu, a Chinese general and military strategist: "Keep your friends close, and your enemies closer." This way, without revealing specifics of your own strategy of *asking* the world for things, strive to improve chances of discovering what potential damage these people have in mind for you.

● **Avoidance:** Stay away from and communicate as little as possible with those who likely would try to pull down or block your efforts to effectively communicate with the world. If you must undergo direct contact with these negative people, such as a so-called "mother from hell," avoid revealing your true dreams or strategies, since such individuals will only try to tear you down.

● **Support system:** While embracing avoidance and deception tactics, or a combination of both, consider actively *asking* for help or suggestions from supportive friends or acquaintances that seem likely to give you much-needed support. This way, you could skip past any notion that "I have to do it all alone, and doing everything by myself would make my dreams impossible to achieve."

CHAPTER SIX

Ask just one simple question

Just one single question, asked by a single unknown person can change the course of world history.

As a prime example, consider the resounding and indisputable success of Levi Strauss, producer and distributor of the world-famous Levi's® brand blue jeans beginning in the 1870s. The garment soared in popularity, especially more than 90 years later during the hippy movement of the cultural revolution of the 1960s.

But this development never would have happened unless a tailor, Jacob Davis, in the small high-desert town of Reno, Nev., had written a single letter to Strauss.

During the early 1870s at a small livery stable in the Old West, Davis invented a riveting system to strengthen denim pants. Lacking the necessary funds to apply for and receive a patent, Davis came up with the idea to write a letter to Strauss in San Francisco.

Essentially this letter asked words to the effect that "can we split the patent fee?"

Upon receiving the letter, Strauss jumped at the chance, perhaps because the fee was far less than $100. So, all because of that single question, Davis benefited by receiving a new partner, Strauss benefited by receiving exclusive rights to a product that sold briskly for generations, thousands of garment workers benefited by getting steady jobs, and the public benefited when the sturdy, reliable Levi® jeans reached clothing stores.

Yes, like that little-known tailor did well over 100 years ago, today you have the power and the ability to make significant changes just by asking a single question—or, hopefully, lots of them.

Of course, you might lack any unique invention, and the things you hope to ask for might seem insignificant to the world as a whole. All the while, though, remember that a single question can and will spark significant changes in your life, particularly if you remain persistent.

Others can ask your urgent questions

A series of horrible blizzards struck the Sierra in Northeast California during the winter of 1846-47, initially trapping and killing 14 members of the Donner Party while they were en route to what eventually would become the Golden State.

Seven survivors persevered, until finally reaching the other side of the range in January 1847, three months after the horrific snowstorms began. Upon reaching their destination, these initial survivors completed their primary objective—asking that help be sent to those left behind.

The following month, a first relief party arrived before returning 21 refugees to safety. The next week a second relief party found that the 31 remaining survivors had engaged in cannibalism, eating the dead in order to survive.

A primary lesson here is that other people often become necessary to ask vital questions on our behalf, sometimes on extremely important life-changing or life-and-death matters. Such queries might range from our very survival to significant milestones necessary to our perceived quest for happiness.

"Dreams are today's answers to tomorrow's questions," said Edgar Cayce, a widely renowned psychic who died in 1945 at age 67.

A Don Juan character portrayed by actor Johnny Depp, star of many films including "Alice in Wonderland," "The Pirates of the Caribbean" and "Edward Scissorhands," knew instinctively how to put all this into perspective.

"There are four questions of value in life," Depp said in the hit 1995 film "Don Juan deMarco," "What is sacred? Or what is the spirit-made? What is worth living for? And what is worth dying for? The answer to each is the same. Only love."

This emotion, love, can help inspire passion within the soul, the essential seed of self-enlightenment and personal growth, while also inspiring others to ask questions on our behalf. To jump for such chances often means to ask for what the heart tells us is right at the spur of the moment.

Taking such strategies as essential to the essence of life, an age-old saying tells us that "it isn't what you have in your pocket that makes you thankful, but what you have in your heart."

Develop essential will power for motivation

Another potential stumbling block on the proverbial raceway of the Asking Game involves a lack of willpower or insufficient motivation.

We all know people who live life with lackadaisical attitudes, mirroring in some ways what Abraham Lincoln observed, telling us that, "People are just as happy as they make up their minds to be."

Of course, too much of a positive attitude coupled with ample motivation can lead to our demise, like the horrible fate of Capt. James Cook. This officer in the Royal Navy died at age 50 on Valentine's Day in 1775, in a skirmish with Hawaiians. Praised for his boundless courage, Cook's downfall came while making his third exploratory voyage of the Pacific.

"There are risks and costs to a program of action, but they are far less than the long-range risks and costs of comfortable inaction," President John F. Kennedy once proclaimed.

What if you refuse to pick up a phone and issue the one question you think will change your life for the better? How would you feel about yourself, if you decide to avoid sending an essential email requesting an interview for the job that you've always wanted, thinking that "it isn't worth the rejection, since they would never pick me anyway?"

The stories of those who persisted and prevailed are many, sending a signal to all of us that through our refusal to ask vital questions we might be throwing away the possibility of a bright future.

Fredcrick Albert Cook claimed to have reached the North Pole in 1908, one year before another explorer, Robert Peary. Determined to reach that destination first, Cook lacked the type of modern conveniences of warmth and transportation that make such treks relatively trouble-free for many of today's explorers.

Although Cook's claim has remained a matter of intense controversy, he could at least boast before dying in 1940 at age 74 that—whether people believed or not—that he had persevered in a land where no records existed of anyone having traversed before.

Widely acclaimed and popular entertainer Bette Midler sang copyrighted lyrics in the title tune for the movie "The Rose" that "it's the heart afraid of breaking that never learns to dance. It is the dream afraid of waking that never takes the chance. It is the one who won't be taken who cannot seem to give. And the soul afraid of dying that never learns to live."

In this spirit, learn to ask like you've never done before.

Ask, for whatever you need as much as you can, as if your life depended on it. Open up your soul to the possibilities, unafraid and unencumbered—relentless in pursuit of all the many blessings that life has to offer.

Yes, ask, before it's too late, before life passes you by altogether. Take this opportunity to open yourself up to the world, free to cross into a new and exciting realm.

Do you want to travel around the world, but have never done so, afraid to ask the right people about what such planning entails? Are you afraid to ask for a divorce, although your mate makes you miserable and likely will do so for the rest of your life unless that person dies first or you eventually separate? Would you like to enjoy a significant, positive, major life change, followed by the joy such a blessing can bring?

"Once I knew only darkness and stillness," said Helen Adams Keller, a deaf and blind American lecturer, activist and author who died in 1968 at age 87. "My life was without past or future. But a little word from the fingers of another fell into my hand that clutched at emptiness and my heart leapt to the rapture of living."

Persevere, even through adversity

Without a doubt, sometimes life gives us a gift, an apparent unexpected miracle *even when we never ask for such blessings*.

At age 17, George Lamson Jr., emerged as the only long-term survivor among 71 passengers on board Galaxy Airlines Flight 203—which crashed about 1 1/2 miles after takeoff from Reno-Tahoe International Airport on Jan 1, 1985.

"One of the first things we saw was the boy," Reno Fire Department Capt. George Kitchen told the media. "He was still strapped in his seat out on South Virginia Street. He was conscious. We gave him first aid until the medics got there."

Two other passengers who initially survived died from their injuries within a few weeks. The National Transportation Safety Board later listed the probable cause of the crash as "the captain's failure to control and the co-pilot's failure to monitor the flight path and air speed of the aircraft"—coupled with the failure of ground handlers to properly close an air access door. This resulted in an unexpected vibration shortly after takeoff.

Depending on your perspective, luck or fate can also play a major role in whether you achieve your goals. Lamson never had to ask or pray for a god or the universe to save him, for this apparent miracle just happened in a flash.

Just as compelling, consider the case of Anna Conrad Allen, a lift operator whom some rescuers had given up for dead at age 22 after a horrific avalanche slammed through the Alpine Meadows Ski Resort near Lake Tahoe in March 1982, killing seven people. Allen, then known as "Anna Conrad," ate only snow while buried deep for five straight days.

Unexpected word flashed worldwide when rescuers discovered her alive. Frostbite eventually cost Anna the toes on her right foot and her left leg below the knee.

"Well, I came to and was in a tiny hole," Allen later told "Sports Illustrated" magazine. "Everything was pitch black and I had no idea what had happened."

The magazine reported that Allen had begun screaming, asking for help on the second day when she heard searchers some 15 feet away.

Larry Heywood, leader of the on-site, 125-person rescue team, told the magazine that by the fifth day most of his team had given up hope of finding Allen and another victim alive.

"Anna, is that you?" one of the rescuers inquired, when he saw a hand.

"Yes, it's me," came her weak reply, sparking cheers that soon echoed worldwide.

Throughout the ordeal, Allen had hollered as much as her weak body would allow, asking for help from anyone who might hear.

After the rescue officials broke the news to Allen that the avalanche had killed Frank Yeatman, her 22-year-old boyfriend from the University of California at Davis.

Since her rescue, Allen received many blessings in life, thanks largely to what we all possess—an innate and necessary ability to ask for things. She fell in love, married and became manager of a Mammoth Mountain skier safety program.

"I don't dwell on what happened, though it's not something ever far from my mind," Allen told a reporter for the "Tahoe Quarterly" 25 years after her rescue. "One day last spring I was coming home with the kids from skiing. The sun was shining on the mountain all coated with new snow. It was incredibly beautiful and impressive. I smiled the whole way home, feeling like the luckiest person in the world."

Especially for those of us in good health today, Allen's perseverance in asking for help throughout her ordeal serves as a timeless inspiration.

"I never had a question in my mind about whether I would be found," Allen told "Sports Illustrated." "I just felt I would be."

Whether you're facing a severe illness like cancer or enjoy vibrant health today, realize that in this diverse world of more than 6 billion people, many individuals yearn to help us. And remember that we can almost always ask, in some instances even after we have become very weak.

"Look and you will find it," said Sophocles, the writer of Greek tragedies more than 400 years before Christ. "What is unsought will go undetected."

Doomed people should never loose hope

As if to prove the obvious that we never always get what we ask for, pleading for mercy failed to get reprieves for many famous people. Countless numbers of condemned prisoners who held out hope till the bitter end ranged from Mary Queen of Scots in 1587 to Julius and Ethel Rosenberg in 1953.

Certainly, just asking for something never guarantees we'll get what's requested, even though we believe our desires seem just and virtuous. Nonetheless, by at least seeking clemency, people can give themselves some degree of hope, however slim.

In 2008 a DNA test exonerated a 47-year-old man, Charles Chatman, after he was sentenced to 99 years in prison and subsequently served more than 26 years. Chatman became one of 15 people from Dallas County, Texas, cleared thanks to DNA testing. Hundreds of convicts have been released nationwide on the strength of similar science.

"I'm bitter, not angry," Chatman told an Associated Press reporter, shortly before his release from prison. "I'm not angry or bitter to the point where I want to hurt anymore or get revenge."

Like Chatman, many of those who have their convictions overturned were able to achieve those rulings only because they asked for such justice.

"Tomorrow is your big day," the AP quoted Jeff Blackburn, counsel for the Innocence Project of Texas as telling Chatman.

Tales such as these signify that by asking we have hope, by asking we can help bring justice to the world, and by asking we can make our voices heard—especially when using passion and opening up our hearts.

"Stop the war, now!" hundreds of thousands of rebellious young people chanted, amid street demonstrations nationwide in the 1960s and early 1970s. Some protests erupted in violence, while others remained peaceful. Ultimately, their pleas were heard when the war finally ended in 1975.

Unlike during the social revolution of the mid-1900s, today many who seek to protest during presidential visits to their communities get designated to fenced-off free speech zones. Many complain that such bureaucratic rules cut their ability to ask in open public for their opinions to get heard.

Today, the things you might want to ask could range from personal matters that preferably should be kept private among people you know, to major social issues you hope the world will recognize.

"Don't trust anyone over thirty," anti-war activist Jerry Rubin said in the 1960s, a member of the famed Chicago Seven radical group. Rubin later became a successful businessman, before suffering fatal injuries in 1994 at age 56 when hit by a car while jaywalking in Los Angeles.

As citizens of the United States, speaking our minds while asking for a redress of our grievances has become "the American way." Even so, by issuing requests—especially those involving major public issues—we should know that many will seek to deny what we want.

Speak your mind, loud and clear

"Mister Gorbachev, open this gate!" hollered then-President Ronald Reagan, in West Berlin, Germany, in 1987 during the final phase of his second and last term. "Mister Gorbachev, tear down this wall."

Reagan's bold, open request got fulfilled within three years, with the 1991 fall of the Iron Curtain, a notorious boundary that had divided Europe for 46 years.

Reagan had used his position as the most powerful person in the world to issue open protest at the site, to air his differences in an open public place, and to ask a huge question—essentially issuing a command—that would eventually impact subsequent generations.

Today, especially in this land of so-called free speech, you're in a position to issue major requests although presumably on a much lesser scale than Reagan. As long as your requests refrain from asking for an overthrow of our government and avoid any suggestion of violence against our nation's president, you can issue press releases or give speeches—whatever your race, religion or gender.

"I would rather be exposed to the inconveniences attending to too much liberty, than to those attending too small a degree of it," said Thomas Jefferson, author of the Declaration of Independence and the third president of the United States, who died in 1826 at age 83.

Particularly in matters involving public issues, your degree of success when asking for change likely would hinge on your level of perceived power. The greater your suspected strength or the louder you make your voice heard, the more likely your chances for "success" will be—however just or righteous your perceived cause.

Herein rests a primary challenge, as you learn the many intricacies of issuing your requests in manners likely to get the respect and consideration that your positions deserve.

"If once the people become inattentive to the public affairs, you and I, and Congress, and Assemblies, Judges and Governors, shall all become wolves," Jefferson said. "It seems to be the law of our general nature, in spite of individual expectations."

As your personal quest to learn and improve your mastery of the Asking Game progresses, strive to become strong within your heart and within your convictions.

Upon these truths you can and should build a foundation, a base that represents your personal value system. This way, when the time comes for you to start asking bold and righteous questions, you can and should hold steady and firm in your beliefs, goals and what you want from life.

The justice system gets used and abused

As individuals, as a society, as corporations and even as governments, we often take our need or right to issue requests straight into the court system.

By some accounts, a whopping one million lawyers practice law in the United States, exacting a mind-boggling $40 billion in annual judgments.

Americans seemingly want the right to ask for anything imaginable under the stars, from restraining orders to divorce judgments and huge damages from large corporations. The most heated legal disputes often involve big companies going toe-to-toe with consumer organizations.

"Our wrangling lawyers are so litigious and busy here on earth, that I think they will plead their clients' cases hereafter—some of them in hell," said Robert Burton of Oxford University, an English scholar and vicar who died in 1640 at age 62.

Today, many of the most publicized court cases involve the American Civil Liberties Union, the controversial organization that continually asks judges to grant free speech requests. Meantime, our local, state and federal governments often go after each others' throats in the courtroom while seeking to extract funds from individuals as well.

Compounding matters, citizens coast-to-coast flood small claims courts with suits, frustrated after asking debtors for payments never received.

"I'm going to sue you!" some people yell at each other, angered and frustrated. "I'll see you in court!"

"Fine, go get a lawyer!"

To hear some lawyers, litigants and even politicians, as individuals or as groups who band together as allies, people will always do what they think is in their own best interest.

Lots of people might say otherwise, but there are those who claim that through personal experience they've learned this motto: "Never trust anyone, any person, for any reason."

With so much conflict involved, you might say, what's the point of asking anyone for anything? What's the point of going to court, the point of fighting with lawyers, or the point of entering conflict in the first place?

Well, first off, whenever people ask for anything of value—ranging from the return of an engagement ring to expensive repairs on a car—differences invariably emerge. Even if they honestly try to compromise, litigants often end up disagreeing on money totals, perceived values and even morals.

Many people embrace the age-old adage that "99 percent of lawyers give the rest a bad name." Whatever your personal perception, we'll have to admit and openly acknowledge there's often injustice within the American system of justice.

How often have you heard someone who lost a significant lawsuit issue a statement that "justice prevailed?" To the contrary, it's always someone on the victorious side who makes such a statement; huge percentages of "losers" feel sorely cheated.

Many people use the frequent line that lawyers would have a hard time making a living if people behaved themselves and kept their promises.

Keeping these various factors in mind, realize that for you, seeking justice through the court system might very well become an option in the Asking Game. Unless you're served with a summons that leaves no other option, you may very well need to decide if such a route would ultimately be worth the price, money and potential heartache.

Get the RESPECT You Deserve

CHAPTER SEVEN

Learn how to get people to like you

For most of the 1900s through today, many of the world's acclaimed teachers of interpersonal relations have stressed the need to listen to others.

Authorities of interpersonal relations, including Dale Carnegie, author of "How to win friends and influence people," stressed the importance of asking questions.

Most people have at least one sense of superiority over you. So, always remember that asking questions and especially listening to other individuals can serve as an effective way to make them feel important.

By asking insightful, continuous and natural questions, you can enable others to speak to their heart's content. This, in turn, might very well make them inclined to like you, since finally—in a sense—these people have someone interested in honestly listening to what they have to say. Among positive and important methods to make this happen:

• **Sincerity:** Show sincere interest in what this person says, genuinely eager to listen.

• **Variety:** Become interested in people, whatever their social status, while varying questions to a variety of topics.

• **Personal:** Avoid getting too personal if the person seems leery of your questions regarding his or her life.

• **Learning:** Show strength to the degree necessary to allow the person to know that he or she is teaching you something of value.

• **Tranquility:** Avoid voicing unnecessary disagreements with people you know or that you've recently met. Conflict tears down trust, rather than building solid relationships.

Added to this mixture, show genuine happiness upon meeting people once again, smile to convey that you like something about them, and remember their names. While striving to learn what interests a person, admit when you're wrong about things without putting yourself down—always cognizant of the importance of remaining kind.

Help solidify your friendship by stressing the areas where you agree, and also allowing people to reach their own conclusions. While always remaining cognizant of each person's individual perspective, tell stories in order to forcefully convey or dramatize your opinions rather than making short, logical statements. This way, you'll come off as accommodating and an easy person to become friends with.

Throughout these interactions, asking regular and persistent questions will remain a key to your success in developing solid or fulfilling relationships.

Develop an inquisitive mind

The age-old saying "curiosity killed the cat" fails to hold true when relationships get involved, at least to a degree in most circumstances. Surely as human beings we crave to interact with one another, and learning the hopes and desires of others—while sharing your own personality—can emerge as an essential part of being alive.

"You can make more friends in two months by becoming more interested in other people than you can in two years by trying to get people interested in you," said Carnegie, who died in 1955 at age 66.

As you engage with people in formal or casual environments, always allow everyone to maintain their dignity. Showing an appropriate amount of praise can go a long way to solidifying relationships.

The Asking Game process remains essential for all this to happen, especially when employed in a sincere, caring and natural manner.

Major changes will result for those who've rarely asked other people casual questions about their beliefs or what's happening in their lives.

What about you in this regard? To this point, have you focused most conversations on yourself, rather than focusing on others? When chatting with your spouse, co-workers, relatives, friends and acquaintances, do you step up interaction by inquiring about their lives?

Perhaps you speak very little if at all to others, especially if you're shy and innately believe—perhaps wrongly so—that you lack the ability to communicate. Well, a great way to get past this hurdle is to begin asking naturally flowing questions in an easy, unpretentious and spontaneous manner. Many people find themselves surprised to discover this system of social interaction clicks into gear with little effort.

Tell your story, while also asking questions

A former Nebraska farm boy, Carnegie became broke and ended up living in a New York City YMCA in 1911 at age 23 after trying to work as an actor. Penniless, he got the spark of an idea to teach other people how to speak in public.

But amid the first lessons Carnegie ran out of material, so he asked or encouraged students to start speaking to others in the class about anything that made them angry. This request opened proverbial floodgates, as speakers became unafraid to tell their opinions.

Herein rests a key, an integral strategy of getting people to open up and speak their minds as you ask them vital questions. Discover what ticks off each individual, specifics on what makes that person upset. By letting others do most of the talking you can open up their souls, creating opportunity to form a solid bond.

All along, respect the person's virtues, as if you wished that you possessed similar traits. Rather than doing this through deception or unethical behavior, strive to look at situations from this other person's point of view. Asking integral questions helps convey such sentiment.

"Any fool can criticize, condemn and complain, but it takes character and self control to be understanding and forgiving," said Carnegie, who developed an institute that graduated nearly a half million people by the time he died. Dale Carnegie® Training still thrives, helping people everywhere learn important relationship skills.

A natural expert in human interaction, Carnegie gained fame in part by teaching us that people crave recognition. Indeed, most people dream of some sort of achievement or advancement, the notion that something can take them another step closer to their perception of happiness.

Using this philosophy as solid bedrock, start today by asking questions of people you already know or even of new acquaintances. "Associate with men of good quality if you esteem your own reputation, for it is better to be alone than in bad company," said President George Washington, who died in 1799 at age 67.

By asking natural, non-intrusive questions of people you know, and of those acquainted with them, you can discover clues into an individual's character. The amount of fun or excitement involved depends largely on your perspective or the frame of mind you choose to take.

"I want minimum information given, with maximum politeness," said former First Lady Jacqueline Kennedy Onassis, who died in 1994 at age 64.

Dull people avoid asking questions

Have you ever been invited to someone's house for dinner or met a person for a first date in a restaurant, only to have them avoid asking anything about you?

Many observers insist that "people are most concerned with themselves;" we sometimes find ourselves disappointed or even hurt emotionally when other people focus only on their lives—while ignoring ours.

Using an imaginary situation as an example, consider what happened to Ruth and Paul Cardington, an Omaha, Neb., couple who invited their new neighbors for dinner

From the moment Charlie and Janet Sloan arrived at the front door, these guests talked non-stop about their own hectic lives. Giving the Cardingtons little opportunity for interaction, the Sloans gabbed without letup about their previous home in Cleveland, every boring detail of their arduous move and even Janet's quest to find an appropriate hairdresser.

When Ruth Cardington finally finished serving desert, the Sloans were jabbering without letup about the intricacies of Charlie's high-paying job as a technical writer for an aerospace company. Finally, as the Sloans eased out the front door at the end of their three-hour stay, they asked the Cardingtons if the couple wouldn't mind taking care of their dog Barney the following weekend.

"Did they ask a single question about us?" Paul asked Ruth, the moment they were left alone in their living room.

"I don't know for sure, but all I know is that we're never inviting those people over again—ever," Ruth said, stomping into the kitchen to start washing dishes.

Paul followed her, and he immediately started helping his wife with the chore, commenting that: "It's amazing how people often show little interest in each other. Too many people seem self-absorbed with their own lives. Don't you agree?"

"We see people all the time like that, Paul, you know the Williams and the Webers—the type of folks we would prefer to avoid if we could," Ruth said, loading the dishwasher. "Life's too short for us to allow self-centered folks like that to waste our valuable time. I only wish we had never agreed to take care of their stupid dog."

Those who fail to ask questions suffer

Meantime, as the Cardingtons started their dishwasher and sat down in the living room to watch TV together, next door the Sloans ripped open a bag of puppy food to feed little 8-week-old Barney, a shepherd mix.

"That was great of the Cardingtons to agree to watch Barney next weekend," Janet said. "We hit the jackpot when we got neighbors like them. They seem like good people."

"But we don't really know anything about them," Charlie said. "Those people might be ax murderers for all we know. Heck, they sure seemed quiet, didn't they? They didn't say a single thing about themselves."

"Some folks just prefer not to speak much about their own lives," Janet said. "I'm sure they must be fine people, and I hope we become good friends. We'll have to invite them over here for a barbecue in a few weeks."

A moment later the Sloans shuffled off to their bedroom for the night, unaware that by this point the Cardingtons had pretty much written them off as potential close friends.

If the truth be told, the Sloans are wonderful people. However, individually and together they lack wholesome, interactive people skills. Neither feels fully comfortable when talking to other people and Charlie especially feels somewhat awkward the moment a one-on-one conversation ends—as if he lacks any inkling of what to say.

Well, on schedule the following weekend the Sloans flew to San Francisco for a four-day motivational seminar co-sponsored by his employer, the aerospace company. In keeping with the firm's policy,

Janet tagged along with Charlie to several of the seminar's sessions, where family cooperation is often mentioned as integral to inspiration.

Both got quite a surprise on the seminar's third day, when the luncheon speaker was the widely acclaimed author of a hot-selling book about the importance of asking. This speaker drew plenty of applause and a one-minute standing ovation. But for the most part Janet kept her mind focused on Fisherman's Warf, where Charlie had promised to take her for the afternoon.

As the banquet ended, representatives of Charlie's employer passed out complimentary copies of this hot-selling book about the importance of asking for things. The remainder of the trip went well for the Sloans, who enjoyed lots of fun in San Francisco. Janet gave the book little thought until immediately after their trip ended.

Bored soon after takeoff during their return flight home, Janet pulled this book from her purse and began reading. At her side Charlie slept the whole way home, while she became engrossed by the many positive stories about the vibrant success of movie stars, the Donner Party, world renowned inventors, hassles involving lawyers—and especially vital suggestions about asking through the remainder of the book.

"You have to read this," Janet told Charlie, on their way home from the Omaha airport in a cab. "It's crammed with amazing suggestions, important things that could change our lives for the better."

"But it's just one book about asking, honey. Come on, give me a break."

"No, please, honey, I'm telling you this could work for us, opening up new doors in our personal lives and for your career."

Thanks to Janet's persistence, Charlie finally relented, unaware that these lessons would spark a profound, positive change destined to transform their lives for the better.

Ask your relatives positive questions

The next evening, Charlie breezed through the book within three hours while Janet went to the movies with her relative—a second cousin, Blanche—who lived in Omaha. Charlie had already tucked himself into bed for the night and was just falling asleep when Janet returned home.

"Did you read that book?" Janet asked in a half-whispered voice, as soon as she entered their bedroom. "Don't you think it was pretty good?"

"Yeah, it was okay," Charlie said, rubbing his eyes and turning on his side so as to avoid light streaming in from the hallway. "The second half of the book was even better than the first."

"Golly, it's amazing how many questions we ask in life, isn't it?" Janet said while hanging her clothes in the closet. "But do we ask the right questions of the right people? And do we ask for enough of the best things in life? It's an interesting concept."

Without getting an answer, Janet realized that Charlie had already fallen asleep—snoring as usual—by the time she gently eased into bed beside him. As Janet closed her eyes, she wondered for a moment about their new neighbors, the Cardingtons, who impressed her as wonderful people.

The next morning while sitting at breakfast with Charlie in their dining room, Janet posed a question that she had been thinking of since their return home the previous afternoon: "Honey, why don't we use our new neighbors, the Cardingtons, as guinea pigs while studying the impact of that book?"

"What do you mean by thats?" Charlie said. "I've got to leave for work now, or I'm going to be late ... Use them as what, guinea pigs? I don't understand."

"You know, maybe we could use some of those strategies about asking questions to bring those people out of their shells," she said, sipping coffee. "Those people seemed so reclusive when we went over there for dinner; they barely mentioned themselves."

"Fine, fine, but I've got to run now," Charlie said, standing up and putting on his sports coat. "I've got a meeting with my new boss, and I don't want to be late."

Show persistence to fine-tune your asking skills

Late that morning, Ruth Cardington answered an unexpected knock on her front door while Paul was away playing golf with buddies.

"Hello, Ruth!" Janet said, smiling broadly, far more so than she had done on her previous visit to this residence. "I'm so happy to see you again. I'm here to get our little friend, Barney."

"Oh, isn't he a cute little guy?" Ruth said, acting appropriately friendly and polite but thinking inwardly that she had hoped to avoid this new neighbor as much as possible—since life is too short to spend time with people who care only about themselves.

"I have so many questions to ask you, Ruth," Janet said, still smiling and holding out a large fresh chocolate cake she had baked just one hour before. "I don't know anything about you and Paul. You seem like such wonderful people. You don't mind if I come in for just a few minutes to visit, or I can come back later."

"Well, I...I," Ruth initially stuttered while taking hold of the cake, and then she let her intuition take hold. "I didn't expect you this soon, but sure, sure, come right in."

Smiling often and using a natural, friendly tone, Janet fired off a virtual shopping list of insightful questions during the next three straight hours. To this point in life, asking so many questions of anyone was out of character for Janet. But she did it anyway, still using lessons from the book as sort of an experiment and hoping to draw Ruth from her apparent cocoon.

Janet allowed Ruth to do most of the talking by far, as the women shared egg sandwiches, fruit salad and a few cups of tea while little Barney played with a beach ball in the back yard. Each woman took delight in discovering they shared many common interests, from going to high-rated arts movies to enjoying long, leisurely evening walks.

Finally, at just before 2 o'clock in the afternoon, the women hugged goodbye after agreeing to go to lunch together exactly one week later, before taking in a movie. A few hours after Janet left, Ruth gave Paul a big bear hug the moment he returned home from his golfing excursion.

"Paul, I was wrong about the new lady next door—she's already one of my brand new best friends," Janet said, giving her husband a quick peck-kiss on the cheek.
"What? You mean those people next door who don't give a crap about us?"

"Wait a minute, let me explain, they really do care and..."

Powerful
lifestyle stratagy

CHAPTER EIGHT

The process of asking permeates society

Always remember the fact that the importance of asking remains essential to the success of personal relationships. And, keep in mind that tens of thousands or perhaps millions of people nationwide are paid to ask questions and listen to answers—before making decisions.

The ability and need to ask essential and concise questions plays a key role to the success of police officers, journalists, lawyers, researchers, writers, teachers, corporate CEOs, doctors, nurses and many other professionals.

Without exaggeration this skill reigns supreme for professionals who must ask insightful questions in a timely manner, queries that often involve matters of life or death.

For instance, a 911 operator who fails to ask critical questions such as the location of a shooting or the number of assailants risks the lives of victims and police. Paramedics responding to potential fatal incidents must ask precise, urgent questions the second they arrive on scene. Failing this, people could die.

Out of necessity, our society requires vital questioning skills among judges, politicians, and news editors—before they make vital decisions. Can a lawyer's client, a murder suspect, get released on bond? Is a politician willing to start a vital new social program after hearing pleas for improvements or change? Where will an editor decide to place a story, if at all, after asking reporters for initial details on a developing crime scene?

In many of these instances, those who must consider vital questions and ultimately make decisions are swayed by the persuasiveness of people who give answers or who pose questions as well.

In one of the most famous cases involving those paid to make decisions on significant questions, in 2000 the U.S. Supreme Court ruled on a pivotal Florida vote count dispute. George W. Bush became the nation's 43rd president as a result, after jurists agreed with the arguments of his persuasive team of lawyers.

"A culture is made or destroyed by its articulate voices," said Ayn Rand, a noted screenwriter, novelist, philosopher and playwright who died in 1982 at age 77.

For the most part our higher education systems lack such courses entitled "Asking 101," although these essential skills play a huge role in the nation's overall quality of life. Some journalists admit that although they received sound college educations, they never were offered courses on the art of developing and asking questions.

Walter Cronkite, the legendary journalist and retired anchorman of the CBS evening news, born in 1916, has been quoted as saying that "I think it is absolutely essential in a democracy to have competition in the media, a lot of competition, and we seem to be moving away from that."

Sure enough, numerous major media companies reported sharply lower earnings revenue as the first decade of this century waned, while newspapers and TV networks made broad and sharp cutbacks in their corps of journalists.

Support the educations of those who must ask for us

For our society to progress on a positive path, we must remain diligent in training people from a broad spectrum on how to ask the right type of questions. Only after making such inquiries in an insightful and effective manner can these professionals develop workable and economic solutions to today's most serious problems.

All along, we should never assume that asking appropriate questions is easy. Only via research can scientists and even police pinpoint minute details or finite problems in certain cases. Today's most formidable challenges go far deeper than just the surface of primary problems, from climate change to a global economic crisis.

As the younger generations learn to dig deeper into the dynamics of today's most pressing issues, they'll need to press further than the mere surface of what new professionals must learn to ask.

Many seasoned experts who are paid to ask questions need to dig deep, when inquiring about the primary basic questions—"who, what, when, where, why and how," skills they must hone as their careers mature.

Elizabeth Dole, a Republican and former U.S. Senator from North Carolina, has been quoted as saying that, "What you always do before you make a decision is consult. The best public policy is when you're listening to people who are going to be impacted. Then, once a policy is determined, you can call on them to help you sell it."

Advertising and public relations enter the fray

Considered by many analysts as the backbone of our economy, the advertising and public relations industries generate hundreds of billions in annual revenues.

For the most part, their job is to ask you—the consumer—to purchase, notice, invest in or use products and services.

Here again, an entire industry moves due to the importance of asking. It's as if almost every person and company within our society hinges its success or failure on the ability to ask. And for the most part, that's true.

Advertising industry executives and members of their creative teams stand to bring home paychecks, small or large, based on their success or failure at asking you to buy, attend, get involved or join something. Some of these firms get paid big bucks by huge companies such as firms within the pharmaceutical industry.

Collectively and individually, the advertising and publicity businesses strive to avoid falling into the type of quagmire mentioned by President Abraham Lincoln: "What kills a skunk is the publicity it gives itself."

When effective, though, a publicist or advertiser's successful ability to ask you a question before getting an affirmative response can reap massive profits for clients.

"I have always believed that writing advertisements is the second most profitable form of writing. The first, of course, is ransom notes," said Philip Bernard Dusenberry, a widely acclaimed advertising executive who died in 2007 at age 70.

Wayne Rollan Melton

The Internet expands, improves and complicates

Steadily since its introduction into the mainstream public in the mid-1990s, the Internet has expanded, improved and complicated the entire process of asking—especially in matters that involve advertising and public relations.

From Facebook.com to MySpace.com and YouTube.com, a massive new interactive universe has been born. Advances move with such lightning speed that even some of the most knowledgeable nerds find trouble keeping pace with the need to learn.

Some observers have said flat-out, according to ThinkExist.com, that, "It shouldn't be too much of a surprise that the Internet has evolved into a force strong enough to reflect the greatest hopes and fears of those who use it. After all, it was designed to withstand nuclear war."

Therein for all the world to observe are cyberspace sites where surfers can meet and fall in love, locate houses and cars—and possibly end up undergoing an online quest for divorce attorneys. Each day, hundreds of thousands of people ask for buyers on eBay, while people frequently email friends or acquaintances they haven't seen in years.

All these many technological developments and societal challenges permeate deep into each of our lives. This leaves individuals with pulsating, relentless questions, initially for themselves and eventually for others:

• **Venue:** What is the best venue or method for us to ask specific types of questions?

• **Message:** What specific type of text or words will get us the best results?

- **Time:** What is the ideal time to ask questions, so that we'll get our desires fulfilled?

- **Targets:** Who are the people we should submit our most vital questions to, and how can we locate them?

- **Passion:** What's the appropriate and most effective level of personal energy to use?
- **Ethics:** Where is the line you'll never cross, regarding honesty and openess?

When delving more deeply into this realm that involves asking life-changing, pivotal questions, you'll learn to focus on these factors. Then, those who choose to do so can begin a process destined to change their lives forever.

Now, are you ready to join them?

Even so-called experts can "fail" when asking

With an ego larger than Manhattan, Doctor Leo Marvin gets frustrated by a patient in the hit 1991 film "What About Bob."

Conflict intensifies when Bob Wiley, played by Bill Murray, starts pestering the shrink and his family as they strive to enjoy a one-month vacation on a lake in New Hampshire. Played by Richard Dreyfuss, Doctor Marvin begs, cajoles and even demands that Bob leave the property—but always to no avail.

Unperturbed, Bob intrigues and entertains the doctor's wife, Fay, daughter, Anna and son, Siggy. Movie audiences roared in laughter, especially each time the psychiatrist failed in asking this odd man to leave.

Bob emerged as a huge annoyance to the doctor, who wanted to pitch his book about personal development on ABC-TV's "Good Morning America." This movie's plot intrigued many film fans, especially the notion that a supposed expert in human behavior lacked any ability to get a "yes" answer from his patient.

"Insanity—a perfectly rational adjustment to an insane world," observed R.D. Laing, a widely acclaimed Scottish psychiatrist who died in 1989 at age 61. Laing once described human beings as bemused and crazed creatures, strangers to their true selves, to one another and to the spiritual and material world—"mad from an ideal standpoint we can glimpse but not adopt."

Even for so-called experts in human behavior, herein rests the challenge of successfully getting other people to give us what we ask for in all aspects of life. Ultimately, what is the importance of asking a question, and when or how should that be done?

Underneath these timeless challenges rests a constant predicament. As individuals, groups and communities, we strive for many of the same objectives amid limited resources or positions.

Success here comes down to the fact that each question you ask is essentially some form of a sales pitch. In just about every significant aspect of life you're selling everything from ideas, objects, services or skills to your spouse, boss, friends, relatives, acquaintances and even to people you've never met.

"For every sale you miss because you're too enthusiastic, you'll miss a hundred more because you're not enthusiastic enough," American motivational speaker Zig Zigler has been quoted as saying.

The perennial hit TV series "Survivor" launched in 1992 enables viewers to observe a microcosm of what human beings struggle for in striving to get what they want. "The Apprentice" television franchise launched in 2004 chronicles just as much struggle within the jungle of humanity, especially when business magnate Donald Trump tells contestants "You're fired!"

Mirroring at least some vital aspects of life, TV programs such a these stress the need to ask vital, insightful questions—before striving to behave or perform in a manner necessary to achieve what you are hoping for from life or from others.

Famous for his negotiation and personal relations skills, Trump has been quoted as saying that "sometimes by winning a battle, you'll find a new way to win the war."

Those of us striving to improve the effectiveness of how we ask for things should take such advice to heart. The key to success in getting "yes" answers often hinges on understanding the basics of human behavior.

Once you accomplish this, enjoy a potential universe of boundless benefits. Here, a primary first step often involves taking a full survey of the world around us. Only then can we jump to the necessary level of understanding, the playing field where our various queries motivate others to give in to the many requests that we make.

Examine the entire world of prospects

By some estimates, at least 261 people will be born worldwide during the time it takes you to read this page.

That's right, streams of people keep pouring into the world, most positioned to eventually ask just as many insightful questions as you are today. Complicating matters, many of these individuals and those already in the adult stage will seek the very things you want.

For you, the trick will be how to position yourself within the realm of the world population, which the International Programs Center at the U.S. Census Bureau estimates will have surpassed seven billion individuals on Oct. 18, 2012.

The vast majority of the estimated 54,810 people who will be born while you read this book got here because one or both of their parents asked a question—either verbally or by their actions, essentially saying: "Will you spend intimate physical time with me?"

If the late American showman P.T. Barnum was right, that "there's a sucker born every minute," then only 210 of this type of individual will have been born during the time you get from the first page of this book to the last. That would leave more than 54,000 to take advantage of the rest.

While these various statistics might seem on the surface as mere mindless fun or fascination, they actually drive home an important point. Everything comes down to the fact you're in a big competition at this very moment.

Streams of other people will want—or already crave—the objects, services, jobs or recognition that you desire. Within your own limited universe and throughout the world as a whole, you're locked into a significant competition.

Like it or not, the likelihood of getting what you desire has hinged on your ability to ask with effectiveness in your life thus far. This factor should grow in importance during your future. Any failure to improve this skill could prove significant to your happiness.

George Bernard Shaw, an Irish playwright who died in 1950 at age 94, injected appropriate humor into this predicament, when observing that "if more than 10 percent of the population likes a painting, then it must be bad."

Such light, airy observations fail to take away the fact that so far in life, it's likely that you've failed to get or achieve many of the things you've wanted. You can and will enjoy greater success after initially observing the worldwide and local social environment, and then honing your skills at requesting the things that you desire most.

Look at the world around you

Stop for a moment and take a good, calm and tranquil look at the world around you, throughout your everyday environment.

Other than plants, undeveloped earth, the sky and clouds, virtually everything your eyes behold is here because someone asked for it. Pay attention to the pavement on the street, the concrete in the gutter, houses, buildings and anything else that people made.

Putting this into perspective, the actual page you're reading now was created because someone wanted it, they asked for it to be created.

Virtually every manmade thing you've ever touched, from baby diapers as a child to the favorite clothes you've owned as an adult was requested by someone. While all these factors might seem obvious, more people could benefit along with you if they took time to fully understand these basics. The process involves far more than just the economy.

Those of us who possess superior abilities of asking can position ourselves to get, create or distribute these "things" — benefiting ourselves financially.

On an even deeper level, everything you see that's manmade also was created thanks to human nature, coupled with the fact consumers felt they "needed" these objects. By understanding the desires people hold in this regard, you'll learn to switch the necessary trigger buttons required to get consumers, friends or relatives to respond.

Also become a master of human emotions

Another massive scale involves virtually every person you already know or will meet in the future. This aspect of the Asking Game involves peoples' individual basic human or biological emotions and desires, everything from hunger and cravings, to the yearnings for physical intimacy.

You can achieve your own dreams by effectively appealing to these various emotions within others. By learning how to ask and to eventually satisfy their yearnings, you'll become a master of everything they want—thereby getting your requests fulfilled.

The legendary Beatles song "Money can't buy me love" in the 1960s became an international hit record. The message might seem logical and indeed such a theme holds true in a large sense. Even so, as you'll soon learn, there are many ways to control, manipulate or magnetize the emotions of others depending on how you ask. And, yes indeed, money can magnetize people, though that's not necessarily the primary focus here.

Either other people want you to make them feel a certain way, or conversely you're the person who wants them to respond to your requests. Certainly while honing these skills, you'll increasingly realize that the Asking Game is invariably a give-and-take situation.

Your success or failure hinges on your abilities to master these variables, the interface between the physical, biological and emotional realms. To understand these complexities, you must first evaluate your current situation to determine how the process has worked so far in your life. From that point you'll become positioned to master this intangible craft.

Consider your current situation

At this very moment, everything about you and where you are hinges on questions that you have asked of yourself and of others.

Whatever your perspective, you have placed yourself into your current situation as a result of your own choices—coupled with the questions you asked and answers received.

For instance, the clothes you're wearing now—if any—ended up on your body because of questions you asked and eventually the decisions made by yourself or others.

Intermixed with fate or luck, your spouse or lover—if any—entered your life due to questions you asked of yourself, of that person, and of the universe around you.

In order to put this overall situation into perspective, consider just some of the many factors involved in your life. Among them:

• **Finances:** Your personal money situation hinges largely on everything you've asked for ranging from a job, an education, a lottery ticket or from a variety of other potential sources. The "success or failure" of these requests generated your current results.

• **Home:** Based partly on your finances, the roof over your head today—if any—came into your life due to a wide variety of questions you've asked. Lifestyle choices played a big factor. You've considered locations, architecture and design either by asking for specifics or by refraining to ask for details—letting the universe help make the decisions for you.

- **Community:** Today, you're in a particular town, city, state or country either by deciding to move there or by preferring to stay put in that environment.

- **Knowledge:** Everything you know now hinges on what you've decided to retain from your experiences through the course of life so far. What schools did you ask yourself or others to pursue for you? What classes did you ask for and decide to take? What learning-related questions did you ask of yourself and of others? What knowledge did you decide to retain or to forget?

In these areas and many others, results hinge on questions you've asked of yourself and of others, coupled with fate or chance. Realizing this, the types of questions to pose when conducting a self-assessment now might include such queries as:

- What places did I ask myself about going to that resulted in meeting my spouse or locating my current residence?

- What lovemaking options did I ask myself about that resulted in the births of my children?

- If I'm unemployed today, did I ask myself certain questions about education in the past that played a role in my current situation?

- If I'm overweight now, have my inner questions about health and lifestyle emerged as motivating factors? In recent years many people have started acknowledging the beauty of sensing and appreciating what we experience in the present moment. As your life progresses, you might want to consider asking yourself how your future "now-moments" might change considerably if you ask different questions of life.

Sometimes you never ask vital questions

Your decision to avoid asking key questions of yourself and of others also likely played a big role in getting you where you are today.

For instance, out of fear or preference, you may have avoided asking yourself openly about the possibility of leaving your spouse or finding a new mate. Out of fear or from indifference, you might never have seriously asked yourself about the possibility of moving elsewhere. The number of options seems boundless.

Indeed, the questions we fail or refuse to ask of ourselves and of others play as large of a role in how our lives evolve as the queries that we consciously decide to impose.

So, as your life progresses from this point forward and as you hone your skills in the Asking Game, deciding to ask new types of questions plays a huge role in creating potential change.

As your tactics, strategies and results in the Asking Game improve you'll be deciding what new types of questions—if any—to knowingly and purposefully start asking yourself. When your level of self awareness increases, you can open a new realm of possibilities. Among potential options:

● **Home:** If unhappy with your living environment, will you start asking yourself about the possibility of moving?

● **Work:** If unhappy with your current employment situation, will you start asking yourself about options that could generate change?

● **Finances:** If you've never seriously considered or pursued new types of revenue sources, will you start asking yourself a wide variety of questions about other potential options?

Ultimately, the decision on whether to ask and eventually pursue such choices will hinge on your personal desires, level of motivation and values. The good news for you today is that potential possibilities are likely to unfold, once your mind and spirit become increasingly cognizant of everything that life's Asking Game entails.

You're continually asking questions

Whether you're cognizant of this or not, everything you do, think, say or decide to avoid is asking questions of the world, of yourself and of others.

For instance, the clothes you're wearing now ask the world to perceive you in a certain way. If you're wearing tattered blue jeans with many holes in them and a ratty 20-year-old shirt, the world is asked to perceive you as perhaps poor, sloppy or mega-casual. By wearing a sharply pressed, neatly fitted business suit, you ask the world to perceive you as a professional with perhaps an educational background and financial resources.

The way you speak asks the world to perceive you in a certain way. For instance, if you continually intersperse unnecessary phrases such as "you know" and "ahhhh" in your vocabulary, you're asking the world to perceive you as an unpolished speaker—perhaps uneducated and possibly as a person who cares little about what others think.

James, a 35-year-old man with washboard abs and shoulders as firm as bowling balls asks the world to perceive him as healthy. Barring health-related issues that might have caused the problem, Marcus, a fellow of the same age who allows his belly to sag over the beltline asks the world to perceive him as caring little about a healthy lifestyle.

Of course, many physical attributes or lifestyle placements occurred as a matter of chance, such as the body that nature gave you or the family you were born into within a certain economic segment of society. As life progresses, we decide which of these attributes to keep or maintain in order to ask the world to perceive of us in a certain way.

For instance, Darlene, a seriously obese 22-year-old woman who is otherwise healthy decides to eat too much, pushing herself 124 pounds above her ideal weight. Meantime, Darlene's identical twin sister, Henrietta, stars in the Joffrey Ballet. Darlene asks the world to perceive her as uncaring about health, while Henrietta wants to be perceived as talented, energetic and dedicated.

Yes, barring unforeseen forces such as accidents and natural disasters, we either consciously or unconsciously ask the world for things at every given moment.

Tried-and-True

System

CHAPTER NINE

What are you asking for right now?

Without a doubt what we ask the world for, either intentional or un-intentional, plays a big role in eventual results from the universe.

James, the healthy looking man mentioned earlier got an unexpected offer for a high-paying, lucrative modeling contract. Meantime, Marcus, the seriously overweight gentleman was turned down after an in-person interview for a low-paying, boring clerk job.

David, a recent law school graduate who asked himself as a teenager about the possibility of becoming a lawyer landed a good position at a fairly respectable starting salary. During law school, David had asked himself how to improve his grades and to expand his contacts within the legal profession. As a result, as a student he decided to pursue a seasoned mentor already within the profession, a choice that lead to his first professional advancement.

Julie, a 40-year-old graphics designer, complains that she can never find steady work although many of her equally talented friends within the profession often land lucrative employment in the craft. Sadly,

Julie fails to realize that she's asking the world to perceive her as either incompetent or a slob. You see, she shows up at interviews wearing wrinkly, ill-fitted and soiled clothes.

Yes, the many things that we consciously or indirectly ask of the world play a huge factor in determining what we'll receive.

Adam, a highly motivated college basketball star who sets an all-time scoring record for one season in his league asks the world to consider him as a potential high-paid candidate for the National Basketball Association.

Conversely, his equally skilled teammate, Jamal, often warms the bench. Jamal lacks motivation or desire necessary to win. Adam asks the world to perceive him as a winner, while Jamal comes off as a "never-was."

Our individual and personal attitudes, energy levels and pursuits collectively and individually all ask the world for specific results.

Those of us who ask the world for a so-called negative outcome are likely to receive just that. And those of us who ask for positive results position ourselves for advancement, in everything from our personal lives to our professional careers.

Value systems play a key role in what to ask

Adam, the successful basketball player, values money and fame enough to receive them. His no-scoring pal, Jamal, craves those things as well, but not enough to ask for them in the form of a passionate, admirable on-court athletic performance.

Marian values peace and quiet most in her life, so she has asked life-style questions that resulted in her getting a home in a tranquil high-mountain meadow. Her sister, Hannah, values blaring rock music and fast-paced social excitement. So, Hannah asked for, pursued and received a job as the manager of a popular band.

Invariably our value systems play a huge role in the questions we develop and ultimately choose to ask or to avoid asking.

Martha values a loving relationship with a man, far more than she values a professional career. So, at least for now, Martha refrains from asking herself to seek a high-paying dental hygienist job that she's qualified for—bowing to the wishes of her husband who wants to move to another community.

Conversely, Travis leaves town to accept a lucrative job that he actively asked for at a big-name advertising firm. Although Travis feels deep love for his girlfriend, Olivia, he never seriously asks himself to stay with her or to ask her to come along because to him the relationship has less value than the job. Desperately in love with Travis but unable to go with him due to her college commitments, Olivia weeps hysterically as he leaves—asking and even pleading with him to stay.

Value systems also play key roles in questions that couples ask of themselves and of each other. On a Sunday morning, Kenneth and his wife, Patricia, agreed that later in the evening they would make love after dinner. Then, Kenneth spent the day working upstairs in his home office, creating the latest images for a newspaper cartoon strip.

Finally, at the appointed time following a long arduous day of work he came downstairs when Patricia called him for dinner. Patricia frowned the moment Kenneth entered the kitchen, telling him: "I'm not going to make love with a guy who spends the entire day at home in his bathrobe. You change your clothes now, if you want to get intimate with me."

As far as lifestyle, Kenneth valued a relaxed atmosphere at home on a Sunday. But Patricia's concept of necessary and stimulating restful activities before lovemaking entailed a classy, high-end attire for the male.

Knowing this about his wife, Kenneth caved in without arguing. Because Kenneth also valued and craved physical intimacy with Patricia, he acquiesced to her question or command and summarily went back upstairs to change. They eventually spent the night making love.

"Every weekend morning in the summer, I ask my sons to go outside in the backyard with me to play catch with a baseball," said Calvin, a 43-year-old drywall installer. "I'm usually dead tired on my days off. But I value quality and healthy time with the boys more than anything. So I often ask them about activities that they might enjoy."

Different perceptions play a role in ultimate results

Remember what you've just learned about the fact we always ask the world questions whether we realize that or not. Well, an individual's preferences play a key role in how the world responds to these queries.

Monica, a 23-year-old recent college graduate who works in a psychiatrist's office, gets turned off by men who wear snappy business suits for reasons she fails to understand. By contrast, her co-worker, Jennifer, gets turned on at the mere sight of their boss, Kevin, whenever he strolls through the office entry area wearing his typically crisp suit.

Keep in mind that by wearing such outfits, Kevin either intentionally or unintentionally is asking the world to perceive him as a high-class, high-paid professional.

Yet as far as sex appeal Monica perceives such clothes as a major turn-off. Overall, for the most part she considers men who wear expensive suits as overly stuffy and self-centered. Her previous negative experience with another employer played a key role in developing this response.

Jennifer on the other hand craves men with lots of power and charisma, characteristics that Kevin has in almost every regard. Yet because society asks us to remain politically correct at all times, avoiding any intimacy with the opposite sex in the workplace, Jennifer never even hints to the boss that she craves intimate time with him.

The lesson here is that despite the fact we're always asking the world for things, whether intentionally or unintentionally, the way we convey that message is likely to get a variety of potential results.

"Begin to imagine what the desirable outcome would be like," said Maxwell Maltz, a motivational speaker, best-selling author and American cosmetic surgeon who died in 1975 at age 76. "Go over these mental pictures and delineate details and refinements. Play them over and over to yourself."

While considering which messages to convey to the world, from the perspective of basketball star Michael Jordan, *we should not necessarily change who we are or what we want just to please others.* Born in 1963, Jordan has been quoted as saying that "if you accept the expectations of others, especially negative ones, then you never will change the outcome."

Consider possible results before taking action

Start off this quest by remaining cognizant of the urgent need to consider possible results. A swift assessment of potential outcomes before asking questions seems essential. In order to grow and prosper into maturity and financial security, a person must view an entire spectrum of possible outcomes. To do otherwise seems foolhardy.

Malcolm, a 35-year-old professional singer, fell a bit behind one year in paying his federal income taxes. The next year he planned to catch up with the obligation, using income due from a touring Broadway show company. But funds never came, and he either forgot or neglected to tell his wife, Monica, about the problem.

Although this talented entertainer gets applauded as a good, enthralling person with a kind heart, Malcom's mind usually remains focused on what he calls "non-worldly matters." He invariably forgot to make his necessary IRS payments during the subsequent year. Monica caught wind of the situation when certified mail arrived from the agency.

Hoping to save face, Malcolm assured Monica that everything would be OK. Then, he spent all of their savings on a beat-the-IRS company that assures positive results. The company summarily lost on Malcolm's behalf. And he ended up getting socked for a tax bill far greater than the original assessment.

Needless to say, Monica hit the roof and threatened divorce when the predicament forced her to get a high-interest second mortgage on their home—high monthly payments because of their poor credit.

Looking back today, Malcolm realizes he could have avoided this heartache if he asked himself lots of questions beforehand: What will be the actual outcome if I fail to maintain adequate tax payments? How can I keep up with this obligation if I fall behind, due to my sporadic income as an independent contractor? How will I handle Monica's reaction?

In observing Malcolm's plight, does his general situation bring to mind negative outcomes in your own life? When was the last time you failed to ask yourself formidable questions about a potential negative outcome? What questions about potential outcomes should you ask yourself now and in the future? And perhaps most important, how and when can you forgive yourself and move on with life?

Many of us embrace the timeless moral, telling us that forgiveness is the scent that the rose leaves on the heel that crushes it. To this end, J.K. Rowling, famed author of the "Harry Potter" book series, has been quoted as saying that "people find it far easier to forgive others for being wrong than for being right."

Some of us display recklessness when failing to ask questions

Brent, a professional process server, spent all his available cash to help a buddy launch an electric hairbrush. The entrepreneur, Bartholomew, verbally promised to cut Brent in on the expected future financial windfall. Naïve and untested in this realm, Brent took his pal at his word.

Patent and development expenses swelled. Although by this time Brent had lost his processing job, he paid virtually all the patent development costs for Bartholomew's company. Horrified and locked with fear, Brent's wife, Jessica, sold their getaway home near Lake Havasu, Ariz., to make ends meet.

Desperate for success, Brent took $14,000 from those funds and moved out. He left Jessica to fend for herself, and this heartbroken woman filed for divorce. The first 12 years of their marriage had been relatively blissful.

Unlike Malcolm, the singer who innocently stumbled into his IRS problems, Brent had been reckless in failing to ask himself vital questions about potential outcomes. Looking back, Brent could have asked himself everything from what would happen if the invention failed to how Jessica would react.

Yes, bad things can and do happen to good people every day, especially individuals who neglect or flat-out fail to ask themselves essential questions. The situation worsens when people with bad behavior also fail to ask themselves questions about potential outcomes.

"Why in the world did I do this?"—Such statements echo as a common question, from countless individuals sent to prison every day for criminal convictions. Embezzlers, con artists, common thugs and the rest of their lot pay a horrible price, a solitary outcome many of them never envisioned.

Mary Surratt wept profusely in July 1865 on the day before she became the first woman executed by the federal government, for her role in the successful conspiracy to assassinate President Abraham Lincoln. Just like three other conspirators hanged at the same time, Surratt died a horrific death when the hangman's noose failed to break her neck.

Immediately beforehand, executioners had forced Surratt and the other three condemned to walk past their newly dug graves. Several months before the executions, some historians claim, while carrying out the plot Surratt had neglected to ask herself about this potential outcome.

A half century after the famed playwright Oscar Wilde claimed there is no sin except stupidity, the mega-genius Albert Einstein put it more bluntly: "Two things are infinite—the universe and human stupidity and I'm not sure about the universe."

Even if such assumptions are correct, those of us with normal or superior intelligence can change behaviors, allowing ourselves to start asking questions that were neglected or overlooked in the past.

Realize that you're only human

Take a moment to admit that you've made your fair share of mistakes in the past, and that no matter how hard you try more challenges are likely to arise in the future. The severity of tomorrow's difficulties can be lessened by asking ourselves important questions today.

Those of us with enough maturity and gumption to face up to our past failures in asking things can rebound and prosper. Rather than labeling yourself as an idiot, perhaps you can begin asking yourself, "What negatives can be turned into positives?"

Desperately in love with each other, Jessica and Brent got back together after his attempt to help the electric brush inventor became a total bust. Bartholomew, the inventor, actually blamed Brent for the failure for running out of funds. Rather than dwell on the past, however, the couple focused on ways to ensure their economic survival.

During the year after their short-term separation, Jessica and Brent each landed fairly good jobs in the public relations division of a lumber mill. But that July the couple got laid off by a shady con artist who owned the plant; he refused to issue their final paycheck.

Near penniless and lacking a solid, steady income, Brent landed a side job using his superior carpentry skills. As an independent contractor, he worked steadily from August through October remodeling the kitchen of a prominent physician. Payments from the doctor trickled in well past the times that they were due, while Jessica and Brent barely managed to pay their bills.

Then, in mid-November a dream awakened Jessica in the middle of the night. Her inner senses told her that in order to prosper financially together, she and Brent needed to ask themselves many sensible questions.

"Brent, we need to turn the many negatives of the past into positives," she told him during breakfast on the morning after her dream. "We need to ask ourselves what we're good at doing, and how we can use our best skills to become self-sufficient."

Open to change, Brent spent the entire day with Jessica as they asked themselves many questions about their best, most lucrative working talents. Each agreed that Brent possessed exceptional, vastly superior carpentry skills, making him capable of fashioning the type of unique, hard-to-get kitchen and bathroom cabinetry that's in strong demand.

Working in their garage, by Christmas he created an easy-to-replicate, assembly line system to generate high-end cabinetry. Meantime, Jessica used her superior video and Internet production skills to advertise, asking the world to flock to Brent's new business.

At first this venture and the rate of growth seemed relatively slow. But the company thrived by the following June largely because Brent diversified and expanded his product line. His company has remained vibrant ever since.

This couple's success story is just one example of how each of us can push past our failures of asking good questions in the past, and instead position ourselves for potential prosperity by inquiring now about our best personal qualities and talents.

"Take up one idea—make that idea your life—think of it, live of it, dream on that idea," said Swami Vivekananda, a Hindu missionary among the first to introduce yoga in America; he died in 1902 at age

39. "Let the brain, muscles, nerves—every part of your body—be full of that idea and just leave every other idea alone. This is the way to success; this is the way great spiritual giants are produced."

You should also avoid asking questions on occasion

As you become increasingly inspired about the possibilities entailed in asking questions, remain cognizant that some queries might result in negative, life-changing responses.

Popular American TV and movie actor Bob Crane made the fatal mistake of asking women to pose nude for amateur-made films, at least according to various news accounts and police investigators. Crane was found bludgeoned to death in 1978 at age 49 in a Scottsdale, Ariz., apartment building. Later, a jury acquitted a photographer accused in the murder, citing a lack of evidence; the crime has yet to be solved.

Arthur Neville Chamberlain, former Prime Minister of the United Kingdom, became a disappointment to some British subjects. By some accounts, he signed a document committing to peace along with the infamous German dictator Adolph Hitler. The agreement was signed after Chamberlain asked to meet with this Nazi leader through diplomatic channels.

Although many in Parliament continued to hold Chamberlain in high regard, his popularity became stained in the eyes of many due to what some people portrayed as an unwise and foolhardy appeasement to the enemy.

At an airport gathering upon his return to Britain in September 1938, Chamberlain called the document "the prelude to a larger settlement in which all Europe may find peace." Yet World War II erupted soon afterward. Chamberlain died in 1940 at age 71.

Margaret Hamilton, best known for her role as the Wicked Witch of the West in the 1939 classic movie "The Wizard of Oz," apparently had asked a question—but perhaps not forcefully enough. By some accounts Hamilton had asked producers if a trap door necessary for filming was safe. Believing their answer, she suffered severe burns when her costume erupted in flames during filming of an exit scene from Munchkiland.

Another question apparently posed by Hamilton resulted in an answer that might have shocked or offended some actors. According to at least one account, and reportedly stories Hamilton later told in a humorous tone, while the "Oz" film was in pre-production, MGM Studios called this actor's agent and told him of their interest in the possibility of her acting in the film.

"Oh, I loved reading those books to my kindergarten children. Which role?" Hamilton asked her agent.

"The witch."

"The witch?" she asked, apparently stunned.

"Yes, what else?"

Tales such as these drive home the point that we should refrain from asking certain questions, or at least be sure to pose them forcefully when we do. So, always remember the importance of not asking questions in a willy-nilly manner.

Meantime, however, you should also refrain from allowing the fear of a negative or horrifying answer to hold back your curiosity.
"The important thing is not to stop questioning," Einstein said. "Cu-

riosity has its own reason for existing. One cannot help be in awe when he contemplates the mysteries of eternity, of life, of the marvelous structure of reality. It is enough if one tries merely to comprehend a little of this mystery every day. Never lose a holy curiosity."

Other potential pitfalls also pose danger zones

While cognizant of the various pitfalls that questions can entail, you also should keep on the lookout for an appropriate or politically correct manner to pose your queries. This means avoiding potentially embarrassing times, places or methods.

In Mark Twain's 1876 classic novel "The Adventures of Tom Sawyer," the title character, a 12-year-old boy, asks and convinces other children to whitewash a long fence and take over the chore for him. Lucky for Tom, he escaped serious punishment.

Fisticuffs and a slapping-fest erupt during a barroom scene in "Destry Rides Again," a 1939 film starring Marlene Dietrich and Jimmy Stewart, after various characters get a little too rambunctious in their quest for answers.

Such scenes pale by comparisons to real life dramas, where nosy people ask too many pointed questions, offensive questions, or critical questions of hosts they hardly know. Overly personal inquiries at embarrassing times could immediately lower your rating on the social ladder. Among examples:

● **Finances:** With various other guests crowding a dining room, you ask the host within earshot of everyone about a 120-year-old painting on a nearby wall: "How much did you pay for that?"

● **Mates:** At an intimate afternoon tea with other well-to-do women, you ask one of the most esteemed guests about her husband: "Now, why on earth would you want to marry a guy like him?"

- **Job interview**: While being interviewed for a $175,000-a-year job as a lobbyist, you ask the lead partner of a law firm hiring for the position: "Why does that other law firm down the street have powerful clout, while yours gets nothing but disrespect?"

- **Wedding:** At a wedding reception, you approach an attractive young woman and sit down beside her: "I'd ask you to dance, but I've already noticed you have three left feet."

- **Appearance:** At an arts reception, you approach a man you hardly know and try to act friendly, but in the wrong way: "A guy as heavy as you needs this many hors d'oeuvres?"

- **Aroma:** You're at the backyard birthday party of a friend who lives down the street. You approach her as other people stand nearby. Just then you realize someone has passed gas: "What's that smell, Toni? Is that you?"

While these various missteps might seem obvious or perhaps even humorous at first glance, we still must remain fully cognizant of the words we speak. Offending others should remain off your list of potential ways to advance in life in a positive manner.

"A man's manners are a mirror in which he shows his portrait?" said Johann Wolfgang von Goethe, a widely acclaimed German writer who died in 1832 at age 82.

One of the best ways to gain a reputation as a winner involves knowing when to keep your mouth shut. Keep quiet without saying a word unless you have something constructive, compelling or insightful to say or to ask. And if you stupidly make such a mindless query—and many of us have—remain aware of the need not to blame others when they inadvertently do the same.

"When a man points a finger at someone else, he should remember that four of his fingers are pointing at himself," said Louis Nizer, a widely acclaimed Jewish-American trial lawyer who died in 1994 at age 82.

Use caution when people ask you questions

While honing your questioning skills, remain aware that other people might not have honorable or innocent intentions like yours. So, beware or at least become somewhat cautious when answering their questions—especially queries that might seem overly intrusive.

In fabled tales of long ago, within various cultures the Big Bad Wolf has often been represented by a creature that acted friendly on the outside, while hiding selfish inner intentions. The stepmother in the German-inspired fairy tale "Hansel and Gretel" asks or convinces the children to enter the forest where she abandons them.

Wise to her plan, the children leave a trail of pebbles that enables them to retrace their steps to return home. Soon afterward their father leads them back into the forest, but only breadcrumbs are available for the trail. Animals eat the morsels, and the children soon meet a woman who is really a witch.

With a house made of gingerbread and candy, the witch plans to eat the children after fattening them with goodies. In many versions, Gretel ends up tricking the witch into an oven where the woman had planned to cook her.

Many of us remember tales such as these from pre-school and our earliest years in elementary schools. The stories we heard might have been sanitized from the original versions in order to remove any sense of violence.

Deep down, tales such as these give us a clear vision into real-world situations where potential evil-doers try to behave as if they're saintly. One frequent version of the German-inspired fairy tale "Snow White" comes to mind, when the innocent young woman by that name eats a poisoned apple provided by a witch.

Today, because we live in a challenging world, we need to remain alert to the fact there are many people—whether we like this or not—who will seek to take advantage of us.

Brent and Jessica, the couple mentioned earlier who started a cabinet-making business, had been tricked into working at a lumber mill by a conniving owner. This man, Enrique, had asked the couple few questions when hiring them, saying "your positive reputation precedes you. There's no need to ask you many questions." Enrique later refused to give the couple their final paychecks, although they had rightfully earned their salaries.

To this end, you would be well served to heed the advice, "caution is the eldest child of wisdom," words of the famed author Victor-Marie Hugo, creator of "Les Misérables," who died in 1885 at age 83.

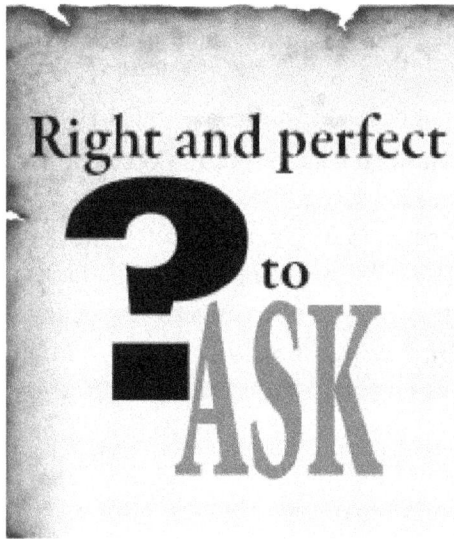

Right and perfect

? to

ASK

CHAPTER TEN

Become an expert at negotiation

As you master the Asking Game, the need to get your various requests granted becomes increasingly paramount. After all, the objective of many queries is to get something you want, usually an object, service, action or a change from existing conditions.

Merely asking a question never guarantees that you'll get the response you desire. So, what's the best way to pose a query in the most effective manner?

The key here is to remember at all times that virtually everything you do is far from merely asking for something. What you're doing is negotiation. That's right, as stated earlier you're always asking the world for things. But at this point you also learn that you're "negotiating" as well.

From the view of many people, a "negotiation" involves at least two groups or numerous people going into a room and arguing until they reach an agreement. Some observers consider this a formal discussion, where one side speaks before the other talks.

According to former U.S. Secretary of State Dean Acheson, who died in 1971 at age 78, negotiation in the classic diplomatic sense assumes the parties are more anxious to agree than to disagree. President John F. Kennedy put the situation more bluntly: "Let us never negotiate out of fear. But, let us never fear to negotiate."

For you as a regular person, when asking questions of other people, governments or organizations, success hinges on your effectiveness in getting down to the core of the issue in everything you request.

Whether you're asking for a soda at a movie theater concession stand or inquiring with a movie producer about featuring you as an actor in a film, you're in a negotiation. Experts at this craft, each of us possesses the qualities necessary to get the things we want.

Most people who teach negotiation skills insist everything in this give-and-take process comes down to three primary factors: *power*, *time* and *information*. Remember these three words because they convey the essence of everything you're learning here.

By mastering the attributes of power, time and information, and employing some form of them in everything that you ask, you position yourself to get the things that you want from life. Remain cognizant of this every time you ask for something.

Without necessarily knowing it, you've mastered these three skills to varying degrees to this point in life. And you're either vaguely or fully aware of the importance each entails.

Fill your queries with power, time and information

For a number of years, these factors have been the focus of people who teach executives how to master the art of negotiation. At this juncture, you're being let in on this "secret" that has played an integral role thus far in your life—and will keep doing so until the day that you die. Once you've got these basics down, you can expand and explode your own brand of the Asking Game of life.

From the perspective of Karl Albrecht, one of the world's richest men and founder of a discount supermarket chain, you should start out with an ideal and end up with a deal.

First off, of course, in asking for things you will avoid telling the person or organization that you're dealing with that "this is a negotiation." Preferably the vast majority of those you want results from never realize there's any sort of give-and-take involved.

At all times, remember that the manner in which you pose questions should convey varying degrees of power, time and information. The essence of each is relatively simple:

• **Power:** Conveys strength and the ability to get things done. By showing the opposite of strength, weakness, you also can get results depending on the situation.

• **Time:** For the most part, this usually entails the period necessary to make a decision. By communicating to your prospects or "targets" that short or long periods are necessary in making a decision, you can squeeze people into responding the way you want—or avoid having them make a choice if that's your goal.

• **Information:** These are the details involved in making a decision. By giving too little or too much information, you can control the negotiation—thereby giving yourself the power necessary to achieve success.

"You may easily play a joke on a man who likes to argue—agree with him," said Edgar Watson Howe, an American editor and novelist who died in 1937 at age 84.

Out of such light-hearted tactics, you can have fun embracing and understanding these three vital factors to the point that they make you an expert at asking for things.

Understand the essence of power

Power is always involved every time you ask someone for something. Having a lot of this attribute or even a little can play a huge role in determining your probable success. Among the many examples of conveying that you have power:

• **Money:** Hold a wad of $100 bills in your hand, while innocently telling a bellman: "You wouldn't have time to take my bags up to my room before all these other customers, would you?" The bags end up in your room in a flash.

• **Celebrity:** You refrain from saying a word to your airline hostess, but the mere fact you're sitting next to one of the world's hottest movie stars seems to do all the talking for you. Your drinks and food are served in a quick, friendly manner.

• **Image:** A thank-you letter that you send on your personal letterhead has a high-class, top-end design conveying elegance and strength. Your invitation to the next party arrives in a flash, a gathering that many high-power executives likely will attend.

• **Sex appeal**: A husband and wife have agreed to physical intimacy late one evening. The wife gets disappointed when her husband still has his bathrobe on during the middle of the day. She briefly brushes up against him, saying: "I've got what you want, so change your clothes now if you want anything precious."

• **Charisma:** Donald, a public schools superintendent holds a press conference, touting charities the teachers have supported. As TV cameras roll, he conveys a sense of power. Beforehand, Donald had encouraging teachers to have hundreds of children cheer for him from the audience. Televisions viewers who saw the cheering youngsters flooded the charities with donations.

• **Strength:** Every time a low-level executive places a call, he has a secretary dial and make the initial contact before saying: "Please hold. Mister Smith is on the line for you." Some people get a sense he's important, thereby inspiring them to bite onto his sales pitch.

Depending on the type of situation involved, conveying a sense of being *powerless* can prove just as important as being powerful. Among examples:

• **Avoidance:** "Charlie is sick and can't come to the phone. He asks that you please call back later after the weekend." Of course, Charlie never wanted to talk.

• **Spending:** Janet doesn't want to pay for this week's luncheon with her girlfriends, so she intentionally leaves her purse in the car: "Sorry, I forgot my wallet. It's back at the office. Can I catch this next week?"

• **Travel:** David wants to avoid paying for the gas on this weekend's trip to the lake with his buddies: "My car is in the shop, Hal. Can we just go now in your car, if that's OK?"

• **Unprepared:** Howard failed to prepare a necessary speech for a weekend business retreat, so he told his bosses that his laptop got stolen at the airport: "I'll just have to wing it."

● **Family:** Donald's mother wants him to fly home to California from New York for Thanksgiving. Not wanting to go, he fibs to mom and tells her: "My girlfriend cried and told me she wants me to stay here in order to meet her family. I want to come and see you mom, but I didn't have the heart to tell her 'No.' I love her so much, and hope you want me to be happy."

Most or all of your queries can or could convey a sense of having lots of power or little power, depending on the situation. These varying levels of strength become particularly effective when intermixed with the other two factors, time and information.

Make "time" a factor to increase the fun

When learning these techniques here, you'll undoubtedly recognize some tactics from your everyday life experiences, but which usually get little attention. Such time-tested skills rarely get spoken about openly, almost as if most people have difficulty describing the process.

Among the most readily recognizable factors is "time," how to use this aspect of life in negotiation, especially when asking for something.

One primary tactic is to employ time with the aspect of power, in order to increase the potential for success when posing a question. Among primary examples:

●**Sales:** "Come on down and get these bargains before Friday night at 10 o'clock. After that, the prices will go back up forever. So act now." By employing this strategy, a sales person adds the aspect of power because prospects must hurry, or otherwise they'll miss out on low prices.

● **Hurry:** While rushing out the door for an important appointment, Jonathan tells his wife, Betty: "You need to make a decision now, within the next two seconds. The only time for me to buy your opera tickets is on the way to the office. I want you to come. Please, will you go?" Squeezed by time and Jonathan's essence of power, Betty feels she has no choice but to say "Yes" although she had hoped to think of an excuse not to attend.

● **Stall tactic:** Michael receives a phone call from a college basketball recruiter who secretly remains unsure whether to sign him. Rather than make a solid offer, the recruiter says: "The draft isn't for another eight months. There's no need to worry now. We still have plenty of time if we ever want to start reaching an agreement."

● **Realty:** Lena, a real estate agent, wants to squeeze an offer on an $825,000 duplex out of Timothy, a wealthy client: "Timothy, my associate—Belinda—tells me she's preparing an offer from the Cartwright Family on the house you want to buy. The Cartwrights are eager to buy the place, and their offer will be ready for the owner tomorrow morning. David, we can beat them to the punch, if you make an offer tonight. OK?"

As a fun, informal test during the next week or so, try employing the aspects of power and time—separately and intermixed—when asking questions for things you want. Fine-tune your queries to determine what tactics get the best results.

Many people who consciously use such tactics for the first time end up telling themselves: "Why didn't I openly think of these methods before? Somehow I've innately known about them for as long as I can remember, but until now I've never used them as part of a well-thought-out plan."

Licitly-split, the aspects of time and power can bring exhilarating energy to the Asking Game. Before long, like many people you might find yourself starting to ask questions just for fun, partly to liven up a situation. Such test-as-you-go strategies, with a free-flowing and relaxed manner, can enable you to stretch boundaries that you might have set for yourself in the past.

Those who reflect upon these basics realize that the aspects of power and time are hinged in virtually every question. Ultimately, many queries—each designed to accomplish various goals—sometimes become necessary in order to fulfill a specific objective. Lots of people achieve their best results by allowing their imaginations to run wild while developing unique questions.

Heinrich von Pierer, a widely acclaimed German manager born in 1941, has been quoted as saying: "There will be hunters and hunted, winners and losers. What counts in global competition is the right strategy and success."

Add information to your repertoire

The information that a person, company or organization has in its possession can play a significant role in the Asking Game. Those involved can use data or the perceived lack of info to convey either power or of being powerless. Those keenly aware of this factor can learn to significantly boost their advantages and odds for success.

Start thinking of the unlimited possibilities in this regard, while reviewing just some of the countless potential examples:

- **Delay tactic:** Hoping to stall off the need to make a decision on whether to buy a dishwasher, Robert tells his wife Inga: "I'm sorry, honey, but I don't have enough information on comparable prices for us to make a decision now."

- **Delay expenses:** "Listen, Henry, we can't make a purchase offer on the company because we still haven't completed an extensive review of its many assets and cash flow. We just don't have enough information yet to make a decision."

- **Strength:** In an effort to convey great power, Bernice tells her boss: "I know everything there is to know about this position, because I've studied it extensively and worked alongside the person leaving the post almost on a daily basis for the past five years. There's no question my knowledge makes me by far the best person for the promotion, because no one knows as much about the situation as I. It would take anyone else years to catch up."

- **Confusion:** "Mary, please let's hold off. I have no idea how much money they have budgeted for the position. So, I'm not going to be able to tell them now about my salary requirement. I'd be shooting myself in the foot if I asked for only $300,000, if they've actually budgeted $450,000."

Just like time does, information can be employed or manipulated in order to convey strength or weakness. Never forget to consider this aspect as an option.

Inter-mix all three aspects to improve results

Now that you've got the basics down, enter the next phase by realizing the best results often reach full bloom when mixing and employing all three of these factors into every query.

Many of the world's best-known leaders climbed the ladder of success primarily on the strength of their abilities to cause or inspire such manipulation, when asking questions of themselves or of others.

To drive this point home, compare Adolph Hitler of Germany to Mohandas Gandhi of India, vastly different individuals who each gained prominence during the 1930s and 1940s. Hitler became powerful in the minds of many by inflicting horrific violence and widespread destruction. By sharp contrast, Gandhi used an anti-violence strategy in attracting the vast majority of people from entire regions to his cause.

While urging his supporters never to hit or shoot their adversaries, Gandhi played a leading role in achieving independence for India. Hitler's opposite strategy resulted in the rise of—and eventually the fall—of the Third Reich of Germany.

Hitler achieved the perception of *power* and influence after asking his supporters in the early 1930s to assassinate his apparent adversaries. Coupled with Nazi propaganda issued to control the flow of *information*, this resulted in the spread of controlled data among the masses.

The information aspect of Hitler's unspoken *negotiation* with the public let everyone know he was willing to kill all adversaries or objectors on a moment's notice. Such revelations increased the perception of this dictator's *power*. Largely as a result, streams of people eagerly committed their *time* and energy to the National Socialist German Workers Party.

But eventually Hitler's *power* crumbled. His regime disintegrated amid the allied invasion in April 1945 when the *information* system at and around Berlin got cut off. As supply lines and communication systems failed, this despot's remaining supporters lacked the *time* or *power* necessary to get adequate *information*—factors that would have been needed for the Germans to have any success at a rally against the Allies.

Conversely, although fighting his battles through *weakness* or non-aggression, Gandhi gained a perception as being a *powerful* force. *Information* about Gandhi's successes spread and largely as a result many allies took time to push hard for a peaceful solution with Great Britain.

The comparisons between Hitler and Gandhi seem ideal to consider, as you ponder your own strategies in the Asking Game on a much smaller scale, the personal level. Whether you want to assume control of a large corporation or merely buy a house, the same primary pieces are available amid your focus on objectives.

REAP *the* Rewards

CHAPTER ELEVEN

Know specifics of your Asking Game playing field

Pure and simple, the Asking Game has the specific pieces that you've just learned about. Now, you must assess the competition field or game board involved in your own situation.

Within a family environment, the "rewards" on each stage of victory can include love, the adoration of a spouse or lover, food to put on the table, adequate income to sustain a desired residence, the need for entertainment, and many other domestic requirements.

At work, the objectives might seem less obvious, because unless you're in top management the big-picture featuring vital information might not become readily available. Within a typical brick-and-mortar style business, you often must wade through a pool of office politics before receiving potential access to desired objectives. The biggest prizes might include a promotion, a raise, health insurance or more vacation time.

And, when playing the Asking Game in an entire community, state or country, the playing field encompasses an entire social environment and massive numbers of people. Potential rewards range from political victories to successful fund-raising events, or the massive, widespread sale of a new product or service.

Whichever of these fields you play on, immediately before entering a particular game, you should assess the likely competition area. Ask yourself: Who are the people—the players—that I need to approach or knock off to reach my objective? Do I need to talk to a number of people to capture a particular prize? Once I approach the necessary individuals, which tactics are the best to employ?

Many people embrace the notion that luck is merely a crossroads where opportunity and preparation meet. Take heart, though, in knowing that if you're thrown into an urgent Asking Game with inadequate preparation, you can still win your objective by relaxing, going with the flow and using your intuition as a guide.

Overcome with eagerness, you can use the following examples of how to proceed within each type of playing field, details that might serve you well in the future.

Master the home environment

While relationships among relatives or roommates can seem horribly complex, the overall playing field is easier to understand and to manage.

First, you likely know all the players involved, in many instances perhaps even more than each of these individuals know themselves.

And second, you probably have better access to essential information within this phase of the game, than you might get at a business or on a massive social scale.

Adding to your firepower, by this point you probably know the triggering points within each of your various relatives or roommates. You realize what inspires them, what ticks them off, what makes them happy and what they crave—plus perhaps vital information important to them and the amount of time they have for various activities.

In addition, you sense or know how powerful each player is perceived within the family unit. This key information can enable you to manipulate or play off each person's sense of power.
Just as important, you likely have specific information or at least a pretty good assumption of everything from finances to the logistics of how and when your family gets its groceries or the other necessities of life.

In a sense, within this arena of the Asking Game, you're almost the coach of a visiting football team—except in this instance you're fully aware of every likely move or reaction your adversary will make. Better still, this opponent might even emerge as a solid ally, essentially putting you on the same competition squad.

Despite these many advantages, however, a potential disadvantage rests in the fact you might want or desperately need all these people in your life—or the realization that many of your most important requests in the past have resulted in heated battles. Even so, rest assured that using the tactics you're learning in the Asking Game, you'll be able to employ various effective strategies.

"I firmly believe that any man's finest hour, the greatest fulfillment of all that he holds dear, is the moment when he has worked his heart out in a good cause and lies exhausted on the field of battle — victorious," said Vince Lombardi, former coach of the Green Bay Packers professional football team, who died in 1970 at age 57.

Possibilities are Endless

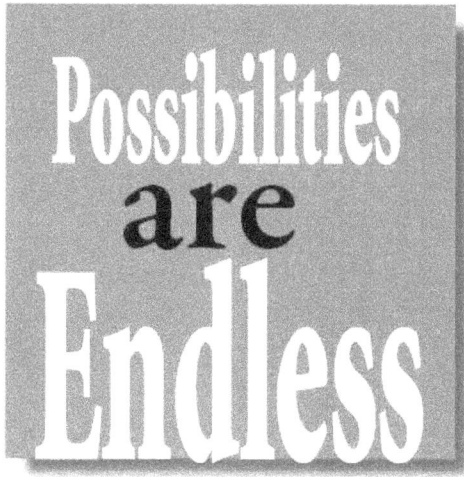

CHAPTER TWELVE

Observe a lively family Asking Game

Clint, a 35-year-old carpenter, had a keen knowledge of his entire family playing field. His wife, Monique, worked hard as a stay-at-home mom in their modest Seattle house, caring for their three children ages 6-12, and he often worked weekends to earn extra cash for living expenses.

Exhausted following nearly 18 months of straight work with hardly a day off, Clint decided he wanted to take a good four-day excursion with his wife for much-needed alone time and solitude. He had mentioned this possibility a year earlier, but Monique balked then, telling him: "There's no way we could possibly leave the kids."

That previous proposal had resulted in a heated argument that featured door slamming, plus a little bit of yelling and crying on her part. To no avail, back then Clint had unsuccessfully argued that they both needed alone-time and rest together, and that he loved her.

This time, Clint became determined to "win," after developing a strategy beforehand. This time, he decided to become as ***powerful*** as possible, to withhold ***information*** from her, and to rob her of any potential ***time*** to say "No."

Finally, after some preparation and cooperation Clint obtained from relatives, on a Thursday morning he drove as scheduled with Monique to drop their children off at their schools. From there, the couple had planned to drive together to a building supply store, where Monique always helped Clint collect and haul supplies needed for his carpentry work.

However, as soon as Clint and Monique finished dropping off their oldest children at their school, he popped a CD into their vehicle's player. At first, Monique smiled oddly and gave Clint a quizzical look as she heard cheering and laughter coming from their vehicle's speakers.

"Hello, Monique, this is your mother—and I want to tell you that you have the best, most wonderful husband in the world," said the voice of her mom, Dorothy. "I want you to know, honey, that everything is set—the children will be fine, OK—while you're away having lots of much-deserved fun."

Just then, while driving the car slowly through a residential neighborhood, Clint magically produced a bundle of fresh flowers, and flashed plane tickets, telling Monique at his side: "This is beautiful, and I love you honey, and we're going to have so much fun—this is going to be fabulous. The bags are packed under the back seat."

Monique began a modest protestation, as her father's voice came onto the recording the very moment that Clint said: "We've only got 20 minutes to make it to the airport, or we're going to miss our plane. We're going to San Francisco for the weekend."

A bit stunned at first and soon enraptured with happiness, Monique began weeping softly as she heard the voice of her father, Bertrand, came onto the recording: "Monique, you're my little girl—a woman now—and I'm telling you, I'm ordering you to have fun on this trip."

Then, one-by-one, the voices of their three children from the CD began cheering and saying sweet things to their mother. Amid this recorded cheering, Clint pulled onto the freeway headed to the airport. The youngsters each told their mommy that they loved her, and finally the children collectively said: "Mommy, have a great time."

Monique ended up on the airplane with Clint seemingly before she knew what had happened. Needless to say, Clint's plan went off without a hitch amid a romantic, fun, restful and exhilarating weekend. For many years that followed, Monique often fondly recalled that getaway as "one of the best times of my life."

Sadly, Clint—this proverbial character—died in an auto accident while driving alone on a country road 12 years after this excursion. His efforts and skills at asking left his family with many fond memories. In fact, Clint had become so skillful at the Asking Game that by the time he died, he owned the primary share of a highly profitable lumber construction company that Monique still maintains—generating substantial income for their family.

Those skilled at the Asking Game
teach vital lessons

Clint had scored a grand slam that weekend. That particular triumph teaches us many things, particularly the fact we can avoid asking the person of our desires—but instead make the vital inquires of other individuals who can get involved in the decision making process.

Besides assuming full *power* in arranging the weekend, Clint showed cooperation and leadership skills. He knew his mother-in-law's *weakness*, the fact that she yearned to care for the children because she loved them dearly. By asking Dorothy in the right way, Clint made her *weakness* part of his strength.

Because his children were essentially penniless or helpless as youngsters, he made that *weakness* his *strength* by giving each a $100 bill—bribing them individually to keep their mouths shut, avoiding the urge to tell their mother beforehand. In this regard, he also controlled *time*, not telling the children until the night before the trip when he secretly took them to their grandparents to make the recording.

In arranging travel, Clint could have picked any one of 12 flights departing that day for San Francisco. Skillful, he chose a *time* exactly one hour after he and Monique were scheduled to drop the children off at school. As a result, he managed to squeeze *powerful* results for himself, because Monique had become *powerless* to say otherwise since she lacked *time* to change her mind before their scheduled departure.

Clint had arranged the weekend within a month after a friend who lived down the street, a successful banker, Hal, became his mentor. The finance expert told Clint early on that "the most important thing I'm going to teach you involves power, time and information."

Clint had learned as a teenager that the old saying is true, that instructors teach us more by what they are than by what they say. To him, the banker seemed the epitome of success. And as Hal would tell Clint, "the Asking Game involves some thought and persistence to become effective."

World
Renowned
SUCCESS

CHAPTER THIRTEEN

Observe the playing field of business

The so-called playing field that involves the Asking Game of business and industry mirrors that of the family in many ways. Like in the home environment, just about everyone involved has his or her individual desires, needs, weaknesses and strengths.

On a much broader scale, however, a business or company often has far more players. The available information can prove difficult to find, especially in a privately owned venture. Also, the times involved often vary extensively for numerous people.

Understandably then, getting a solid grasp on a particular issue can prove formidable when dealing with a business. Some ventures become so large that individual people, or sometimes joint groups of managers or executives, make important decisions.

Depending on the situation involved, the higher-paid executives often are believed to have the most power, while lower-level, lower-paid front-line personnel get classified as having little or no authority in the workplace. Some exceptions prevail, particularly in corporate structures where managers empower staffers to make key decisions.

Proven business models often mandate that only certain people can be approached for specific duties. At a newspaper office, for instance, only personnel in the circulation department have the training and forms to sign up new subscribers.

Einstein made a positive twist to this when he observed that "to punish me for my contempt for authority, fate made me an authority myself." Sure enough, in order to put fate on your side, when dealing with a specific business or industry, you can gain significant power by learning as much as possible about its infrastructure.

"A person who doubts himself is like a man who would enlist in the ranks of his enemies and bear arms against himself," said Ambrose Bierce, an American journalist, writer and satirist who died in 1914 at about age 62. "He makes his failure by himself being the first person to be convinced of it."

Herein is buried the boundless notion that even a persistent underling within a giant or mid-size corporate structure can collect vital, necessary information. Such a strategy proved essential to Clint, well before his death in the traffic accident.

Observe a lively business acting game

At age 38, nine years before he died, Clint still worked as an independent contractor in carpentry. A mid-size construction company on the outskirts of Seattle served as his primary client. The rate of job requests that he received from this company seemed fairly steady for several years. However, suddenly Clint's work orders from the company dropped off markedly, and nobody from management told him why.

Intrigued and increasingly curious, Clint started employing the tactics of *power*, *time* and *information* that his banker friend, Hal, had taught him four years earlier. Amid an otherwise vibrant economy, on the sly—mostly in private—Clint began *asking* as many of the company's management level employees as he could what had gone wrong.

A key supervisor revealed to Clint that the company had begun to fail after one of two partners who owned the business started mismanaging cash flow through incompetence.

Gleaning a vital bit of *information*, Clint learned the firm was on the verge of certain bankruptcy, lacking adequate credit to reorganize and stay afloat—although the company had significant assets such as construction equipment. He learned the *time* of the planned bankruptcy filing, the first Monday of the following month.

Armed with this verified data, which made him *powerful,* Clint met with Hal and asked for a loan to buy the business. Clint had a specific dollar amount in mind, $7.5 million; Clint knew from gathering *information* that this was the minimum amount necessary to keep the business afloat. Despite their friendship, at first Hal was reluctant to entertain the idea since Clint had no significant assets other than his $85,000 annual income and $325,000 equity in a house he owned with his wife.

Cognizant of this beforehand, before approaching Hal, Clint had generated at least five potential partners, each with significant assets and business experience. Clint had established these solid relationships in the previous several years by asking lots of questions of people he knew. People liked his curious nature.

Adding to his *power*, before individually letting each potential partner know specifics of his plan, Clint required nine business people to
sign a non-compete, non-disclosure form. Four individuals he asked
turned down the offer for varying reasons, but he got five to bite
hard.

Clint then asked Hal for a closed-door meeting with this bank executive and the potential partners. Those interested all attended as
promised. On the *strength* of their combined, substantial business
success, Hal and his banking partners felt they were *powerless* to
make any decision other than to grant an immediate loan on the
spot—providing that the construction company's owners would accept the $7.5 million offer.

The next day, a Thursday, Clint put himself in a position of *strength*
by accompanying three of the business people—each well known
within the community—in an unexpected visit to the construction
company's corporate office. Feeling *powerless* because they lacked
time before the following Monday's scheduled bankruptcy filing,
the company's owners accepted the offer on the spot upon seeing
certified banking *information*.

Impressed by Clint's ability to put the deal together with limited
time, the new owners agreed to make him the company's president
and a primary shareholder. Actually, each investor had no choice
other than to agree to this because in advance Clint had written the
contract listing his own name in the top executive position—thereby
granting himself *power*.

Business deals such as these occur every day somewhere in America. Entrepreneurs who show confidence while asking for things position themselves for success, especially when manipulating *power*,
time and *information*.

the perfect PLACE

CHAPTER FOURTEEN

Observe the social playing field

The Asking Game's playing field on a widespread local, regional, state or national scale makes the business and family environments seem to pale by comparison. Potentially hundreds of thousands or even millions of people can become involved.

Since public opinions, preferences, incomes, age categories and educational levels vary, pinning down a specific strategy can become a huge challenge. On this widespread scale the variables involved in the Acting Game get caught up in a juggling act.

The key players range from advertisers and pharmaceutical companies to big-name politicians who all face enormous potential hurdles. Besides difficulties in pinpointing and reaching a necessary target market, extensive funds can become necessary to ask and convince consumers or voters to accept specific requests.

As "Company A" launches an all-out advertising campaign, "Company B" might struggle to keep pace and thereby adopt a vastly different strategy. Failure at this level means the loss of big bucks and possibly prestige.

Legendary American comedian Bill Cosby, born in 1937 and a perennial star of commercials for Jell-o® Pudding and other major brands, has been quoted as saying that "the very first law in advertising is to avoid the concrete promise, and cultivate the delightfully vague."

While most of us will never venture onto this gargantuan playing field, knowing of its many deep and broad intricacies could prove valuable in the long term. Sometimes getting a keen understanding of how the big Asking Game gets played enables us to fine-tune our efforts when dealing on a much-smaller scale.

Notice the aura of the big arena

When running for president in 2007-2008, Barack Obama emerged victorious by amassing real or perceived *power* via the donation of funds—with totals into the many hundreds of millions of dollars, far surpassing previous records.

Along the way, Obama provided voters nationwide integral *information*, which he conveyed in a passionate manner in order to convince them to vote for him. He increased his *power* by giving voters as much of his personal *time* as possible, traversing the country to hundreds of campaign stops at a record pace. He often visited individual locations numerous times.

While debating his opponents, U.S. Sen. Hillary Clinton, D-N.Y., and eventually John McCain, R-Ariz., Obama seemed to win from the view of many observers. From the perspective of some analysts, Obama came off as being *powerful* with a good grasp of *info*, attributes necessary to handle the job. And, Obama's general plan included the *timing* of how to achieve his goals.

Like all political candidates are taught to do, at every campaign stop Obama said things like "I ask you to vote for me;" both novice and seasoned politicians know the age-old adage that "people will not vote for you unless you ask them."

If only on a softer, sometimes more gentle scale, the same holds true for everything from major pharmaceuticals such as Viagra® to big-name soda companies like Coca-Cola®. Many firms try to portray their products as America's favorite, since a majority of consumers deem the most popular products or services as the best.

In exactly the way that these firms and politicians ask their constituents or consumers on a massive scale, you should pose your questions to those within your scope of influence—if only on a much smaller level.

position
YOURSELF

CHAPTER FIFTEEN

Become an actor when asking your questions

Terror and intense fear shot thorough the hearts of Americans in October 1960, when the first secretary of the Communist Party of the Soviet Union, Nikita Khrushchev, seemed to go stark-raving mad during a public meeting.

During a session of the United Nations General Assembly in New York City, Khrushchev went into a wild tirade — yelling and pounding a desk with his shoe. The Soviet leader seemed out of control, leading many U.S. citizens to fear he was a lunatic capable of launching nuclear war on a moment's notice.

Khrushchev became engulfed in a heated yelling match with a delegate from the Philippines. At the height of the cold war, the U.S. and the Soviet Union at the time always remained positioned for possible nuclear battles.

With little doubt, Khrushchev's tirades left many people throughout the west viewing him as a hot-headed tyrant capable of massive destruction. Conflicting news reports about the meeting left many Americans wondering what occurred.

Looking back all these years later, from the perspective of many analysts, while asking questions of his international adversaries, the Soviet leader was actually placing himself in a perceived position of unparalleled power. To some experts in negotiations, Khrushchev was actually a genius. In essence, his tirades were all an act, as if he were a stage star.

A wide range of people, from everyday folks to current world leaders know this about the Asking Game. Many times when we inquire or make demands, our queries get the best and most immediate results when we go into an act—behaving in a pre-planned or spontaneous manner, role playing in order to get what we ask for.

For instance, Khrushchev, who died in 1971 at age 77, made people throughout the west feel hopeless and powerless. Amid his infamous tirades, only Khrushchev had the vital information on whether he actually would launch nuclear war. Skillful in the Asking Game, he chose an ideal time to launch his antics in a significant public forum.

Relentless in his keen skills of igniting fear and trepidation, Khrushchev made other wild statements such as: "Support by United States rulers is rather in the nature of the support that the rope gives to a hanged man." Rather than considering such statements as the mere hogwash of a demagogue, many Americans seriously became upset and fearful.

"To grasp the full significance of life is the actor's duty, to interpret it is his problem, and to express it his dedication," said James Dean, a Hollywood movie star killed in a car crash in 1955 at age 24.

Start acting in life right away

While Shakespeare coined the oft-spoken term that, "All the world's a stage," each of us literally stands to reap huge rewards in the Asking Game if we put on a show in real life.

People highly skilled in this arena know the many blessings of behaving powerful or weak. Some victories come to people when they behave as if truly ignorant of what they're an expert at, or highly knowledgeable of something they actually know little about.

Hannah, a 41-year-old divorcee, cries hysterically whenever Donald—her sugar-daddy boyfriend—threatens to leave her for good. Hannah knows that by showing weakness, she has ***power*** over his emotions.

At well-timed, scattered intervals, some mornings Hannah cries about how much she loves Donald just before he leaves for his job at a finance company. When this happens, she feigns heartbreak, wailing that she's afraid he'll leave her.

But the moment Donald heads out for the day's work, she's happier than a robin during its maiden flight, for her antics have all been a successful acting job. After each of these intermittent tirades, Donald hugs Hannah and vows that he'll never leave her. Like you can do with people you know, she realizes his weaknesses and takes advantage of them.

Jimmy, a 35-year-old video store owner, watched a comedy DVD at 10 o'clock one morning while laughing hysterically right beside his buddies. Half-way through the film, Jimmy's clerk from the front register tapped on his office door, and told him: "That public relations guy you hired is at the front register. The man says he's here to collect his payment."

Jimmy put the movie on pause, before exiting his back office to speak to the PR man, Seth, in the store's main video display area. Jimmy went into a rage as soon as he got there, and immediately started yelling at Seth, saying things like: "That bill you sent was offensive! You're a crook for coming up with a total like that! I'm offended!"

Shocked, stunned and surprised, Seth was unable to say a single word because Jimmy yelled non-stop — robbing the PR man of any possible time to get a word in edge-wise. Seth had never expected this reaction, unaware until then that his bill total had been an issue. Embarrassed and stunned, Seth quickly left, drove away and never contacted Jimmy again.

Moments later, Jimmy returned to his office to resume watching the comedy video with his friend, Louis, who had heard the commotion. Louis inquired, "What was that all about, Jimmy?" By this point, the video store owner had already re-started the movie, laughing at the film as if nothing had happened less than a minute earlier.

"Oh, it was nothing," Jimmy said calmly. "I just didn't feel like paying a bill, that's all. This was just my way of getting rid of the guy."

An expert in the Asking Game for many years, Jimmy had thought up this tactic while driving to work earlier that morning. Only a handful of Jimmy's friends ever knew he employed such role-playing tactics, but that's exactly what he did several times each day — behaving as if sad, happy, grateful or angry, whatever a particular situation dictated.

Are you a potential Oscar® winner?

When many people first learn of such tactics, they step onto high-moral ground, telling themselves that "I would never do such a thing. People like that are as phony as a $2 bill. If I ever end up stooping that low, I'll know that I've truly lost my marbles."

Yet anyone who becomes proficient, versatile and adaptable in the Asking Game realizes that many people are skilled at using such strategies whenever necessary. Instinctively, you might even be employing such strategies on at least a small degree in your life now without giving such behavior much thought. Collectively and individually, our skills in this regard vary widely.

What about you? Would you ever consider employing such acting charades, in an effort to control *power*, *time* and *information*? Well, if you've failed to enact at least some of these strategies earlier in life, still not using them now, you've been cheating yourself. If the truth be told, anyone who has any hope of winning more at the Asking Game needs to grasp these concepts and use them whenever possible.

The various potential character traits span the full gambit of the thespian world, playing lead actor or supporting actor roles in everything from anger and kindness to being aloof, playing stupid, heart-broken or even crazed.

Whether you like to realize this or not, many people are already doing this to you—either "acting" or "role playing," while at least pretending to behave in a certain way. Other people, perhaps lots of them, have been busy playing with your emotions, your needs and desires.

Brian, a wealthy man, actually gets suckered into believing his hair stylist cares about him. Every three weeks or so when Brian goes for a haircut, Bonnie asks him loads of questions about his family, things such as "how is your wife doing?" and "tell me all about your vacation." Brian has actually been going to Bonnie's shop for so long, he has himself believing she actually cares, and he thinks nothing of giving her $30 tips.

In reality, though, Bonnie could care less about Brian, and she actually tells her closest friends horrible things about him, like: "That guy is the biggest rear-end that I've ever met. He's so rude that his mother must have tied pork-chops around his neck to get other kids to play with him as a child."

In reality, Brian is a very nice, likable, intelligent man who has many friends. In addition, Bonnie's employees fail to know this, but she dislikes most people and actually can't stand them. Her actual image is quite the opposite, that of a charming and likable gal. This vibrant, compelling aura plays a significant role in the success of her business.

On a much larger scale, an internationally known entertainer and imitator, Rick appeals to the masses with his on-stage talent, charisma, magnetic smile and likable demeanor while performing. This image gives him power, increasing his fame, drawing approval and personal income. In reality, however, Rick can be a rude smart-aleck with friends and acquaintances, even while dining with them in public places.

Get into the act as soon as possible

Do all these many indisputable assumptions mean that you'll have to behave like someone you're not? Does acting or role-playing during real-life situations make a person phony or the equivalent of a donkey's rear end?

Right off the bat, some people complain as they begin learning these aspects of the Asking Game. Many of us feel we have a right and obligation to avoid creeps who engage in such role-playing. Yet the sad reality remains that, since we're all only human, people are more likely to respond to situations impacting their emotions, fears and needs.

Most specific "acting" situations that you would engage in could entail light degrees of thespian skills that many of us employ naturally every day.

Stephen, a seller of high-end, cutting-edge CAD software used by architects visits the office of a successful firm. To give himself more of a *power* position, the lead partner, Maurice, conveys that he cares little and makes Stephen wait 10 minutes for him in the building's main entry waiting room—taking up valuable *time*.

After waiting in his own office for just the right amount of *time,* Maurice strolls happily into the entry area, smiles and shakes Stephen's hand. Then Maurice walks brisk-paced with Stephen to an employee meeting room, where lots of Mexican food is in large bins atop a long table. Friendly-like, Maurice briefly motions toward the containers: "All this food is still here from our lunch. Sit down, have all you'd like. We won't even charge you for it."

This casual, easy-going comment put Maurice in a greater, barely implied position of *power*. Then, Maurice put himself in a mode of both *power* and *weakness*, looking at his watch while saying, "I'm sorry, but there are things out of my control. Some of our valued clients are showing up here this afternoon—right now, later than they have been scheduled. I'll be back as soon as I can."

Momentarily, Maurice went back to his own office, where he started goofing off on the Internet and calling his wife at home for a few minutes to see how things were going. Actually, no such late-shows had just arrived.

At the same time Stephen began worrying whether he would be able to make this sale; he had other sales appointments that afternoon, leaving him to wonder about the posibility of losing.

At that juncture, each man had differing objectives. Stephen had desperately wanted to make a reasonably priced sale to increase his commission because he was behind on mortgage payments.

Yet this salesman never knew that Maurice and his partners desperately wanted to buy Stephen's product, which features the best software on the market. The firm could easily afford such a purchase, but Maurice's partners strongly suggested a discount price in order to improve their profit margin.

Fifteen minutes after leaving the employee meeting room, Maurice returned just as Stephen began fidgeting nervously in his seat while reading an entertainment magazine. As the firm's lead partner had hoped, Stephen—who had leeway in setting final costs—soon agreed to a rock-bottom bargain price, desperate to make a sale.

By this point, tricked by Maurice's "act" of being disinterested in a possible sale, Stephen felt a need to consummate a deal fast. Stephen felt *powerless* but caved in and gave vital *information*, after Maurice demanded to know the lowest available price while seeming indifferent.

You risk losing unless you "act"

People worldwide—including you—risk losing unless they're willing to act or role-play amid the Asking Game. Stephen's personality is that of a good, kind and generous guy, a person who would never think of offending, lying to or being suspicious of a client. In reality, Stephen easily could have commanded a much higher sales price by undergoing a little role-playing himself.

You see, determined to purchase the best-available CAD software, Maurice had pre-alerted his front office receptionist to fetch him right away in the unlikely event Stephen had attempted to leave the building. Under such a scenario, Maurice's partners had authorized him to pursue the salesman and close a sale—because the company needed the best-available technology as soon as possible.

By behaving as if not necessarily over-eager to make a sale, Stephen would have positioned himself as *powerful*. He also would have retained *power* by declining to reveal the lowest possible sales price, retaining vital *information*. And by behaving as if he had ample *time* to make a sale, he would have made himself as seeming *powerful*.

Adding to the firepower, Stephen could have acted caring and friendly, yet a little more aloof than necessary—perhaps by indicating the possibility of incorrect *information*, that available supplies of inventory for sale were inadequate or unavailable. Here, by seeming *powerless*, Stephen could have gained more strength in this phase of the Asking Game.

Like Stephen had been, in reality, though, odds seem great that people have been manipulating you quite often, without you even knowing it. You see, unless you enter the acting phase of the Asking Game, people and corporations are going to essentially walk all over you—manipulating power, time and information necessary for you to effectively ask for and eventually receive what you want. To do otherwise would be to accept defeat or failure.

While working together preparing for an auction on eBay, because they desperately needed cash, Betty pleaded with her husband, Joseph, to set a lowest-possible sales price of $3,800 in a buy-it-now sale of a rare Indian motorcycle that they owned.

Betty argued that trying to sell for a higher price would be mean and cruel to the potential buyer; she considered the bike as barely worth that much. However, Joseph refused, telling her that selling something isn't a matter of being cruel or kind—but simply what the sales market will tolerate.

Contrary to Betty's wishes, Joseph set the minimum price at $23,000, telling her that "if people are willing to pay that much, that's what it's worth." Two days after Joseph launched the auction, a motorcycle dealership in Albuquerque, N.M., made an instant purchase at the higher price.

Have fun in your acting roles

The greatest, most successful players know that to emerge victorious in the Asking Game, there's little need to get people to truly like them—at least in the sense of being adored and appreciated by everyone all the time.

Still, some of the world's most successful car salesmen write regular hand-written cards to their previous or potential clients. Some of the best sellers tell their prospects "I like you," and much of the time this puts the person in a perceived position of power. After all, who does not want to be "liked" at least in some way?

On an even higher level, superior Asking Game players never get bothered by the notion that some people may end up disliking or even hating them for acting mean. To these players, role-playing is just a necessary strategy that often leads to desired results.

"I don't really care if you make this purchase or not," Emily, a real estate agent, tells a prospective buyer of a $1.2 million home — careful to use a friendly tone. "This is a unique, one-of-a-kind house that definitely will sell, probably fast because it's so rare. I hope you're successful in finding the type of property you want."

From the excited looks in their eyes, Emily knew that she had a few great fish on the hook. Sure enough, the couple — who initially hoped to haggle for the lowest available price — asked her to write up an offer at the asked-for amount on the spot. Earlier in life, Emily never would have dreamed of using such devil-may-care language with potential buyers.

But two years earlier, William, one of Emily's more seasoned associates told her of the role-playing strategy, which has pretty much worked ever since.

Taking this as an important lesson, besides employing the power, time and information in almost every question you ask, always go into "the acting mode" if doing so might ethically help you progress toward your goal.

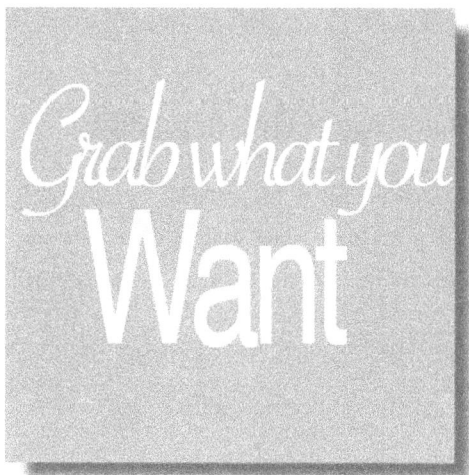

Grab what you **Want**

CHAPTER SIXTEEN

Show courage necessary to ask

As the Titanic sank during its maiden voyage on April 14, 1912, some men asked that their wives and children be put on lifeboats first. Lots of the 706 people who survived showed the courage and gumption to ask their way onto these vessels, knowing that some of them might eventually get labeled as cowards for abandoning ship. Meantime, lots of the 1,517 who perished lacked such gumption.

The everyday trials that you and your family undergo rarely involve such spur-of-the-moment, life-or-death situations. Odds seem great that like many of us, in the past you've been reluctant to ask necessary and vital questions.

Perhaps you were afraid of getting "no" answers or of becoming embroiled in argumentative or confrontational situations. This might seem understandable, because after all, who truly likes unnecessary heated conflict, especially when it's easier to keep quiet and allow events to take their course.

Every day, big opportunities slip past people who lack the gumption to ask for what they want. Some heartbroken spouses, unwilling to lose the love and companionship of their mates, sign away properties that are rightfully theirs. Lots of people pay top dollar for cars, lacking gumption to ask for or to demand bargain prices.

By contrast, those who show gumption position themselves to prosper or at least give themselves a chance for a better life.

At age 19 in 1886, Margaret Tobin broke down and married a poor man, James Joseph "J.J." Brown, because she loved him desperately. Margaret, also known as "Molly," asked herself to show courage in entering the marital union, especially due to the fact that since childhood she had always vowed to marry a wealthy man.

Molly's luck changed dramatically the following decade when her husband's engineering skills made a substantial, positive difference in a mining operation. Although relatively untested in the overall mining industry, he had shown enough courage to ask Ibex Mining Company to use his unique skills and processes. The couple became financially wealthy.

Five years after she and J.J. privately separated while remaining friends, this vibrant woman became one of those who survived the Titanic's sinking—thus earning her famous nickname, "Unsinkable Molly Brown." Well before her time, risking public ridicule, Molly also joined the National American Women's Suffrage Association, which fought for equal rights for females.

Molly's courage in asking many challenging and difficult questions of herself and of society continued during World War I, when she went to Europe during the heat of battle to work with the American Committee for Devastated France. She also spent much of her life fighting for historic preservation, plus the rights of workers and literacy for children.

Today, your individual challenges might seem less formidable, while the need and urgency of showing spunk remains essential. Otherwise, people including relatives and business associates likely will walk all over you—taking advantage—if given the opportunity.

"Never be bullied into silence," said Harvey S. Firestone, founder of Firestone Tire & Rubber Co., who died in 1938 at age 69. "Never allow yourself to be made a victim. Accept no one's definition of your life, but define yourself."

Show firmness while remaining kind and focused

Jeremy performed admirably as an independent contractor, working to rebuild and refurbish classic automobiles for well-to-do clients. During the early years in this profession, Jeremy realized his weakness—failing to press hard to encourage or demand that clients pay him in a timely manner.

On occasion he even personally delivered the completed vehicles to the client's homes. Deep down Jeremy realized that several customers slacked off on their payments, seemingly paying him whenever they felt like it rather than on his terms.

One time he worked three months straight refurbishing a 1956 Chevy, bringing it back to cherry condition. Yet even after dropping off the vehicle at the home of James, a multi-millionaire client, the customer made only sporadic payments every month or so on the completed job. James took a full six months before making the final payment.

A kind and generous, loving man, Jeremy never wanted to push hard for the payments by demanding full payoffs before delivering the

Due to Jeremy's seeming inability to get firm with non-paying clients, his family sometimes had difficulties paying the bills.

That changed big time, fast, when a new client, Winifred, taught Jeremy about intricacies of the Asking Game. Winifred spoke to him about all this for just a few hours, but the lessons stuck and Jeremy has remained grateful ever since. Jeremy learned that he had been too sugary-sweet with clients, that he needed to set boundaries.

Two months after Jeremy fine-tuned his own Asking Game skills, James brought in a 1954 Cadillac for Jeremy to rebuild. This time, when James returned to pick up the car a month later after the work was completed, Jeremy said something he had never told any client during his previous 15 years in business: "Pay me, and I'll be happy to give you the keys."

James whipped out a checkbook and paid the full amount on the spot: "Jeremy, I like seeing you with such spunk. I've never seen this style in you before. You can be sure I'll be bringing plenty more business to you in the future."

Fill your power across the universe

In 1993 a divorced woman contemplated suicide shortly after physicians diagnosed her with clinical depression. Known to her friends as "Jo," this lady barely made ends meet, struggling to live on meager state assistance for herself and her 1-year-old child.

Unable to afford a computer or word processor, in 1995 at age 30 Jo completed the manuscript of her first book on a manual typewriter. Destitute and barely able to afford food, this woman started *asking* publishers to print and distribute her creation.

Twelve unimpressed publishers soon turned down her submission.

170

Undaunted and struggling to keep up hope, Jo *asked* a literary agent to represent her. The green light finally came the following year from a small, relatively unknown publishing house.

Jo's persistence paid off when the 8-year-old daughter of the publishing company's chairman was given just the first chapter to read. The executive knew something was right when the girl essentially *asked*: "Can I please have the next chapter now?"

Soon afterward, Jo got a short-term financial boost when the small-publishing company, Bloomsbury, gave her an advance reportedly in the $3,000 range. The company's editor later remembered advising Jo to "get a day job."

Bloomsbury printed only 1,000 copies of the book in its initial print-run. Little did they know that just a decade later that each one of these first-edition books—individually—would be worth a whopping $35,000 to $60,000 apiece.

At the time, however, Jo was relatively *powerless* in the publishing industry due to her status as an unknown author. So, she bowed to the publisher's request to use initials rather than her full feminine first name of Joanne for the first part of the author's listed name. The distributor had feared that boys would become reluctant to buy the book if they knew the author was a female rather than a male.

She chose the letter "K" as the fictional middle initial, thereafter known to the public as "JK" Rowling. Thanks to her vastly superior writing talent coupled with her persistent skills in the Asking Game, this woman had finally positioned herself for a possible career as a full-time writer.

Before long JK held all the perceived *power*, as the public and publisher began asking her to create follow-up tales to her initial story. Just 12 years later, the seventh and final book in her series, "Harry

Potter and the Deadly Hollows," broke the world record as history's fastest-selling book. A whopping 11 million copies sold in the United Kingdom and the United States on the first day of its release.

According to media reports, Rowling had become a billionaire within the short span of less than a decade, the owner of a luxurious 19th Century estate.

While a vast majority of media accounts chronicling JK's life mention her exceptional creativity and writing skills, for the most part the public hears very little about this woman's faith and persistence in her own abilities within the Asking Game.

Today, at this very moment, you possess similar skills, even if you're conscious and alert but flat on your back in a hospital ICU with nothing but a pen in hand, or homeless on the streets of East Saint Louis. Yes, you can ask, even if only in a simple manner, saying "please" or showing a humble attitude.

Like JK did, you can ask if you're near-penniless, barely lacking enough food to feed your family. You can ask as many people as you're able to approach, and as many people as you want—from the time you awaken till you go to sleep late at night.

You can ask yourself for more faith, for more courage, for more ideas, for more financial resources and even for more peace of mind. Just as compelling, you can ask for ways to help other people, for ways to show your love to the world and to make a positive mark on this planet during your brief time here on earth.

So, will you do that?

CHAPTER SEVENTEEN

Make the Asking Game your true power

Many people have heard common buzz phrases such about "the power of living in the moment," or the "secret to happiness." But in many cases the so-called gurus who espouse such objectives fail to teach specifics on how to make those things happen.

Well, here you've been learning the essential step, the vital need to ask for blessings from yourself and from others. To a great extent, this often involves getting your requests heard loud and clear by those in a position of power to make those vital decisions.

Considered today as one of the world's most influential women, Oprah Winfrey launched her successful career by placing herself into a position of power—rather than having to depend on others to make the most critical decisions regarding her career.

Born in 1954, in the early 1980s following a stint as a TV journalist and host of a low-rated local morning television talk show, Oprah asked herself for permission to "give myself more power." She asked herself for the courage necessary to launch her own company.

As Oprah's countless fans worldwide fully know today, her decision paid off, making her one of the world's wealthiest women and positioning her to become a widely respected philanthropist.

Today, you can ask yourself similar questions, before giving the essence of your soul permission for self-empowerment. Those who want can and will request and absorb the knowledge to enable such personal development to happen.

In 1843 at age 31, Charles Dickens decided he needed to ask himself for the power to advance his writing career. Dickens took matters into his own hands by self-publishing his eternally classic, much-quoted "A Christmas Carol."

"A heart well worth living, and well won," said Dickens, who died in 1870 at age 58. "A heart that once won goes through fire, and water for the winner, and is never daunted."

Embracing a similar strategy, in the mid-1940s while in his late 20s, the owner of a small variety store in Oklahoma asked himself for the power to create many new concepts—in order to make his business unique. As his own boss, Sam Walton gave himself permission to do what few if any other stores did at the time—keep shelves stocked with a wide variety of merchandise at low prices and to stay open longer than competitors.

"I've always been driven to buck the system, to innovate, to take things beyond where they've been," said Walton, creator of the Wal-Mart empire; he died in 1992 at age 74.

Similarly eager to ask himself for ways to seek positive situations, in November 1961 Brian Epstein saw a relatively unknown rock 'n' roll group called the Beatles at The Cavern Club in Liverpool, England.

The following month, Epstein arranged a meeting with the Beatles, and there he asked to become their manager. They signed a five-year contract in January 1962 before catapulting to perennial international fame.

"Well, I don't know about the dizzy height, but I always thought they were going to be pretty big," said Epstein, who died of an accidental drug overdose in 1967 at age 32.

In still another example of how people can ask themselves for ways to achieve, Don Knotts, who portrayed the nervous and beloved deputy Barney Fife in the smash 1960s sitcom "The Andy Griffith Show," faced a dim future as a child when his father suffered a nervous breakdown and died when the boy was just 13 years old.

In 1960, when Don Knotts was 36 years old, he learned that the TV program was being developed. Soon afterward Knotts telephoned his longtime friend Griffith and asked to be considered for the role.

Although somewhat nervous and jittery in his personal life, Knotts placed himself in a position of power by pulling together the strength to ask. The two soon made television history, endearing themselves into the hearts of many generations to follow.

"First they ignore you, then they laugh at you, then they fight for you, then you win," said Mahatma Gandhi, the famed spiritual leader.

All these people who asked to give themselves permission for self-empowerment were just everyday folks just like you.

And just like them, you can continually strive to ask yourself and others for ways to put yourself into positions of power and personal development.

So, when will you begin?

Recruit others to reach those in power

Keep in mind throughout your quest that success in the Asking Game, getting what you desire often hinges on your ability to reach a key decision maker—especially if that person is deemed as powerful.

Many times such people, from corporate CEOs to Little League Baseball team managers, seek to avoid you in order to refrain from having to listen to your queries. The trick for you here is to create a unique method of blasting through the gauntlet.

A potential strategy in this regard often entails recruiting people of lesser power or significance in order to reach the so-called decision maker. Much of the time, the people who work for or who report to this person are considered frontline workers with little or no significant power. Lots of these personnel, volunteers, or organization members fail to realize they're being used as pawns in the quest for development.

Although never officially trained in this tactic, children often employ diverse or adaptable strategies. At 3 o'clock on a Tuesday afternoon, a 5-year-old boy might ask his mother for candy from a jar atop the kitchen cupboards. She refuses, saying "Don't even think of it. You'll spoil your dinner." One hour later, without mentioning the previous request to mom, the child gets some of the treats after asking his father while the mother works in an adjoining room.

As adults, we should always realize that there's never any need to reveal all integral information to people who might grant our requests. In the interim, consider the possibility of having other people ask or appeal to the emotions of decision makers.

In the hit Rogers & Hammerstein musical "The Sound of Music," launched on Broadway in 1959 and later a successful 1965 movie, the lead female character, Maria Rainer, becomes mistress to the seven children of widower Capt. Georg Ritter von Trapp—based on an Austrian who died in 1947 at age 67.

In the film and stage production, thanks to the children's enthusiasm, which she inspired, they help Maria bring a sense of robust fulfillment to Captain von Trapp. Eventually, this man allows the children to sing after he had initially refused to grant them permission to engage in such activities.

Julie Andrews, an acclaimed singer, actor and author born in 1935, and who played Maria in the film, has been quoted as saying that "perseverance is failing 19 times and succeeding the twentieth."

Widely praised for her abilities to cooperate with others, Andrews has told us that "sometimes opportunities float right past your nose. Work hard, apply yourself, and be ready. When an opportunity comes, you can grab it."

A 1963 smash film "The Great Escape" starring Steve McQueen was based on the true story of Allied prisoners of war who attempted a mass escape from a POW camp. Although confined to prison, the men collectively and individually created power for themselves by digging escape tunnels. Asking themselves and each other for ideas, they forged documents and made civilian clothes necessary to survive outside prison.

In the film, only three prisoners eventually escaped after most were captured or killed by the Nazi Gestapo. Viewers got the impression that at least in the sense of their overall quest, the captives achieved victory. Movie fans appreciated these men for at least trying to escape, having the heart and courage to ask each other to carry out tough decisions.

While seeking every day to climb proverbial mountains, crossing into imaginary valleys where your dreams get fulfilled, always ask others for their cooperation—perhaps so that you all can benefit. Seasoned Asking Game winners know that more than one person must act for most major accomplishments to become reality. By asking, always seek to find people who might help you.

"We are all dependent on one another, every soul of us on earth," said George Bernard Shaw, the Irish playwright.

Discover how to get results from "underlings"

While honing and fine-tuning your Asking Game skills, discover that many so-called low-level employees within major corporations often have far more power than you or even they might realize.

At small- and mid-size newspapers, everyday low-paid, frontline reporters make daily decisions on whether to pursue potential stories suggested by public relations professionals. Such decisions often stand to make or break certain ventures, giving events or businesses vital publicity necessary to persevere.

Some unseasoned public relations professionals, sometimes called "flaks" within the news industry, employ the ask-a-lot strategy—calling numerous reporters from a single newsroom until they get a "yes" answer. Such tactics tend to anger or alienate some reporters, who individually or collectively decide to avoid such a person after word spreads about his tactics.

Determined to steer around such potential problems, many public relations professionals strive to establish solid but relaxed and friendly personal relationships with individual journalists. Often this solidifies the give-and-take process, resulting in at least some publicity.

These strategies impact entire communities, front-level employees from a variety of businesses ranging from department stores to food stands.

Taking this further, the most experienced and seasoned public relations pros suggest ideas on a priority basis. These professionals pitch only those potential stories that they know are more likely to be considered as newsworthy.

When dealing with any business or organization, always ask as many questions as possible in order to eventually contact a high-level decision maker. And by issuing a complaint, whether justified or not, you can place yourself in a position of power and thereby get at least someone to listen to your message.

Among other potential methods of conveying power:

• *Empowerment:* Issue a press release yourself, getting straight to various news organizations or directly to companies or individuals you want to pitch.

• *Image:* Hire a seasoned graphics design and marketing person or company to create a logo for you, your business or product. Develop an image that conveys a sense of power, essentially saying that you're "someone impressive or substantial that they should want to deal with." By displaying such an image in everything from envelopes to letterheads and business cards, you're silently asking the world to consider you or your venture as significant and powerful.

• *Persistence:* While careful to avoid becoming a pest, continue to ask as many companies or businesses as you can.

• *Diversify:* Create more than one product, appearance venue or message, partly in order to spread your power base while establishing what seasoned business experts call "an efficient economy of scale."

Multiple products or services that on an individual basis each perform moderately well could collectively generate substantial revenues or goodwill.

- *Internet*: Use every available Internet tactic to get the message out to ask for what you want, from a presence on FaceBook.com with many friends to blogs, message boards and memorable video exposures on YouTube.com.

Always get creative, knowing ultimately that an in-person pitch by you or by someone you want to promote often carries a lot of weight, even in this increasingly impersonal world. Visit a business or someone's home to show that you care or at least possess the heart necessary for them to listen. As they say, "Persistence is the key."

Herein we should always embrace the long-held belief and value system that dictates, "We are not put here on this earth to see through one another, but to see one another through."

Indeed, as stated by Orison Swett Marden who founded "Success Magazine" in 1897, "No employer today is independent of those about him. He cannot succeed alone, no matter how great his ability or capital. Business today is more than ever a question of cooperation."

Long after Marden died in 1924 at age 74, those highly successful in the Asking Game embrace the old proverb lamenting that "we all end up in bed together one way or another."

To this end, even though primary communication methods might change in the coming years and decades, realize that you can overcome potential hurdles by concentrating on, helping or convincing people at the frontline level of almost any organization.

Learn to persevere when people say "no"

At almost every juncture throughout the Asking Game, you'll hear more "no" answers from people than you'll ever be able to remember.

From many of these comments, learn or think of ways to eventually get the answers you want. On an even more important scale, never let negative responses slow, reroute or stop an effort to get the "yes" answers you desire.

Audiences roared in laughter when the fictional character J. Pierrepont Finch learned similar lessons in the smash Broadway musical "How to Succeed in Business Without Really Trying," starting in 1961 and based on a successful 1952 book by that name. The play evolved into a popular 1967 film.

After starting as a window washer for the World Wide Wicket Company, Finch advances to the top of the corporate heap—largely by employing the tactics used by those seasoned in the Asking Game, *power, time* and *information.*

Finch turns down promotions to make himself seem *powerless* when necessary, in order to inspire the sympathies or emotions of others. He conveys false *information* by scattering trash all over his office to make co-workers believe that as a super-dedicated employee he has given their employer excessive *time*, working all night.

Audiences and readers related to such tales without directly being told these were the factors involved. Instinctively, without necessarily having to be told, lots of us know these are the tactics or strategies used in a typical office environment or organization—even all these years later, following widespread corporate downsizing.

Such variables also hold true within the impersonal Internet maze where some co-workers might not see each other at all — working cooperatively on a regular basis for years or even decades.

At a pivotal point in the plot, Finch croons a memorable, catchy tune — the message of which still holds true today more than ever for Asking Game aficionados who must maintain a positive self-image: "I believe in you!"

If you haven't already, gain confidence in yourself starting this very moment. Although you might have suffered through your fair share of failures when it came to asking for things in the past, keep in mind that you undoubtedly have posed some good questions as well. Think about anything positive currently in your life and odds are strong that you probably asked for those occurrences — either directly or indirectly.

In the same way that one critic hailed this musical a "delightful event" shortly after its debut you can succeed at making your personal Asking Game a success. So, feel free to relax and have fun along the way.

Dive in with gusto

Out of passion springs forth flower pedals, opened by questions from bright minds and by those of us eager to swim into a world of this life's unlimited promise.

Brilliant opportunities open to those of us who reveal our hearts, minds and souls to everything great life has to offer. So, enter the tranquility, a peace of mind that emerges when we position ourselves to learn from ourselves and from others.

Gone is the heartache of missed chances, replaced within the Asking Game by new, vibrant and arousing change. With eagerness and avid gusto, we find ourselves able to glide as if doves across a placid pond. The reflection below reveals a willingness to thrive, unashamed of our new appearance as positive citizens of this ever-evolving world.

Through our focused questions, the spirits of others and of our own desires reveal themselves. Humble to the prospects of a vibrant transformation, here rests a chance to move forward with great, penetrating gusto.

By asking, each new day gets impregnated with a mysterious seed, the promise of vibrant, profitable and formidable progress that we've always dreamed of achieving. The process makes the questioner both mystified and fully enlightened.

Indeed, the more we learn when asking questions of the people and of the universe around us, the more we crave supplementary answers — spurring the heart further in a burning quest for more knowledge and for possessions we've always deserved.

As if embracing these sentiments to the core, Oprah Winfrey has been quoted as saying that "passion is energy. Feel the power that comes from focusing on what excites you."

Those who enter the Asking Game with an eagerness to learn and to prosper financially can approach this broad and giving universe with boundless enthusiasm.

"The world itself is the will to power — and nothing else," said Friedrich Wilhelm Nietzsche, a German philosopher who died in 1900 at age 55. "And you yourself are the will to power — and nothing else."

Upon entering the initial orbit through this universe, look for billions of stars each representing what you've always wanted, what you've always needed and what you've always yearned for within your heart—yet lacked the courage and know-how to seek until this precise moment.

"Begin doing what you want to do now," said Sir Francis Bacon, an English philosopher, statesman, lawyer and scientist who died in 1626 at age 65. "We are not living in eternity. We have only this moment, sparkling like a star in our hand and melting like a snowflake."

A tragedy erupts when we fail or lack the gumption to seize every opportunity that we want, in each instance prospects that the Asking Game can provide.

Glistening with the sparkle of life's positive potential, ask now for seeds within your mind and pocketbook to sprout forth—tall, free and at full bloom, opening as if broad, bright flowers spreading for each new day's bright, generous and giving sun.

Health
Money
Respect
Peace of Mind

About the Author

A former editor-on-loan to "USA Today" and an experienced book manuscript ghostwriter, Wayne Rollan Melton has been an entertainment columnist, society columnist and features writer, focusing in part on human behavior issues.

Author's request

Have you had positive experiences in your personal Asking Game, after reading this book? As the author prepares for follow-up publications, please snail mail your comments to:

Wayne Rollan Melton
fixbayinc@gmail.com

Find fulfillment

For details on other books by Wayne Rollan Melton, visit FixBay.com

www.ingramcontent.com/pod-product-compliance
Lightning Source LLC
Chambersburg PA
CBHW031259090426
42742CB00007B/522